LeRoy Rooker, William Gil
& Michelle Mott

AACRAO®
1910

2020 FERPA

FAMILY EDUCATIONAL RIGHTS AND PRIVACY ACT

Quick Guide

American Association of Collegiate Registrars and Admissions Officers

AACRAO® 1910

American Association of Collegiate
Registrars and Admissions Officers
1108 16th St. NW, Suite 400
Washington, DC 20036

Tel: (202) 293-9161 | Fax: (202) 872-8857 | www.aacrao.org

For a complete listing of AACRAO publications, visit www.aacrao.org/research-publications.

The American Association of Collegiate Registrars and Admissions Officers, founded in 1910, is a nonprofit, voluntary, professional association of more than 11,000 higher education administrators who represent more than 2,600 institutions and agencies in the United States and in forty countries around the world. The mission of the Association is to provide leadership in policy initiation, interpretation, and implementation in the global educational community. This is accomplished through the identification and promotion of standards and best practices in enrollment management, information technology, instructional management, and student services.

AACRAO adheres to the principles of non-discrimination without regard to age, color, handicap or disability, ethnic or national origin, race, religion, gender (including discrimination taking the form of sexual harassment), marital, parental or veteran status, or sexual orientation.

LIBRARY OF CONGRESS DATA

Names: American Association of Collegiate Registrars and Admissions Officers.

Title: 2020 FERPA Quick Guide

Description: [2020 update]. | Washington, DC: American Association of Collegiate Registrars and Admissions Officers, [2020] | Includes bibliographical references.

Identifiers: LCCN 2020940314 | ISBN 9781578581269

Subjects: LCSH: Education, Higher—United States.

AACRAO®
1910

2020

FERPA

FAMILY EDUCATIONAL RIGHTS AND PRIVACY ACT

Quick Guide

Table of Contents

About the Authors

LeRoy Rooker

LeRoy Rooker, now a Senior Fellow at AACRAO, is the nation's leading authority on FERPA. As the director of the Department of Education's Family Policy Compliance Office (FPCO) for twenty-one years, he administered laws and policies designed to help protect the rights of America's fifty-eight million students. Mr. Rooker is well known in the postsecondary world because of his extensive outreach to the higher education community. His many appearances at state, regional, and national meetings have been invaluable to the profession and we are honored that he continues to share is expertise through AACRAO FERPA Consulting where he conducts FERPA compliance training.

William Gil

William Gil is the Director of Government Relations for the American Association of Collegiate Registrars and Admission Officers (AACRAO), where he manages and implements AACRAO's public policy agenda and oversees federal government relations, legislative, policy and regulatory matters impacting the AACRAO membership. In this role, he provides information and strategic advice regarding developments in education policy and regulations relating to college admissions, records, student privacy, financial aid and other issues impacting higher education at the federal, state and local levels.

Prior to joining AACRAO, he was the Senior Vice President of Programs and Administration for the Congressional Hispanic Caucus Institute (CHCI), the Associate Vice President for Collegiate Programs and Federal Relations for the Hispanic Association of Colleges and Universities (HACU) as well as a former congressional staffer having worked as the Executive Director, as well as a Legislative Assistant, for the Congressional Hispanic Caucus (CHC).

Michelle Mott

Michelle Mott is Associate Director of Government Relations and Communications at the American Association of Collegiate Registrars and Admissions Officers (AACRAO). Over the past decade, she has helped to oversee the association's policy and advocacy efforts. Ms. Mott is a contributing author of the *Handbook of Strategic Enrollment Management* and serves as editor and contributor to the *AACRAO Transcript*. She is a Phi Beta Kappa graduate of Millsaps College with a Bachelor of Arts degree in history and holds a Master of Arts degree in History and Public Policy from The George Washington University.

Preface

The *FERPA Quick Guide* was written for higher education administrators entrusted with the task of storing, handling and releasing student records. It provides a basic overview of the *Family Educational Rights and Privacy Act of 1974*, as amended, and the full text of its regulations. In addition, this guide highlights how the Act applies to various school officials, including brief outlines of key terms and issues as well as commonly asked questions. It also offers guidance on recent international and state privacy laws, potential issues related to remote work, as well as a comparison of FERPA and HIPPA regulations.

The *Quick Guide* is a useful introduction to FERPA. To obtain a more detailed analysis and application of the Act, as well as extensive FERPA training materials and case studies, refer to the *AACRAO 2012 FERPA Guide*. To order this and other professional development resources published by AACRAO, visit <aacrao.org/bookstore>.

AACRAO FERPA Training Options

For those institutions interested in a more hands-on approach, AACRAO FERPA Consultants are available to help your institution develop policies and procedures for protecting records. AACRAO FERPA Consulting can bring *2020 FERPA Quick Guide* author LeRoy Rooker to your campus to provide your faculty and staff FERPA training tailored to your institution. AACRAO FERPA Consulting is also available to provide an independent third party review of a vendor's product to evaluate its compliance with FERPA. For more information about these services, please visit <aacrao.org/resources/ferpa>.

CHAPTER ONE

Introduction

Under the *Family Educational Rights and Privacy Act* (hereafter referred to as *The Act* or FERPA), students are given three primary rights. They have the right to:

- Inspect and review their education records.
- Have some control over the disclosure of information from their education records.
- Seek to amend incorrect education records.

Essence of The Act

FERPA deals specifically with the education records of students, affording them certain rights with respect to those records. For purposes of definition, education records are those records which are 1) directly related to a student and 2) maintained by an institution or a party acting for the institution.

FERPA gives students who reach the age of 18, or who attend a postsecondary institution, the right to inspect and review their own education records. Furthermore, students have other rights including the right to request amendment of records and to have some control over the disclosure of personally identifiable information from these records.

FERPA applies to all educational agencies and institutions that receive funding under most programs administered by the Secretary of Education (34 C.F.R. 99.1). Almost all postsecondary institutions, both public and private, generally receive such funding and must, therefore, comply with FERPA.

Institutions must annually notify students currently in attendance of their rights by any means that are likely to be read by students. The most common examples are found in the student handbook, catalog, student newspaper or via email. This notice also applies to any students pursuing education via distance education or any other non-traditional educational delivery processes. (*See* Appendix D, on page 107, for a sample of a model annual notification statement provided by the Student Privacy Policy Office.)

The regulations do not specify the means to be used for annually notifying students regarding their FERPA rights. Schools are not required by FERPA to notify former students of their FERPA rights. Although it is highly recommended that each institution publish its annual notification on its website, this method is only acceptable for fulfilling the annual notification requirement if all students are required to have personal computers or are provided with free and convenient access to computers that can access the institution's website.

If every enrolled student is given an institutional email address, schools may send their annual notification via email to their students.

Institutions may not disclose information contained in education records without the student's written consent except under conditions specified in The Act. An institution is not required to disclose information from a student's education records to the parents of dependent students but may exercise its discretion to do so. It is the responsibility of an institution to ensure that information is not improperly disclosed to the parents of students.

To Whose Records Does The Act Apply?

FERPA applies to the education records of persons who are, or have been, in attendance in postsecondary institutions, including students in cooperative and correspondence study programs and in any non-traditional educational delivery processes, such as distance learning.

FERPA does not apply to records of applicants for admission who are denied acceptance or, if accepted, do not attend an institution. Furthermore, rights are not given by FERPA to students enrolled in one component of an institution who seek to be admitted in another component of a school (*e.g.*, a student, admitted to one college within a university, but denied admission in another college, does not have any FERPA rights in the college which denied him/her admission).

To What Records Does The Act Apply?

The Act applies to all education records maintained by a postsecondary institution, or by a party acting for the institution, which are directly related to a student. Records containing a student's name, social security number or other personally identifiable information, in whatever medium, are covered by FERPA unless identified in one of The Act's excluded categories (*see* "Education Records" [on page 15] for excluded categories).

To Which Institutions Does The Act Apply?

The Act applies to all institutions that receive funds administered by the Secretary of Education. This funding can either be in direct grants to the institution or to students attending the institution (financial aid). The Act applies to the entire institution even if only one component, *e.g.*, department or college, of the institution receives such funding.

Enforcement and Penalties

Responsibility for administering The Act is currently assigned to the Student Privacy Policy Office within the Department of Education. This office reviews and investigates complaints, whether brought by the affected eligible student or otherwise brought to the attention of that office. When a violation has been found, the SPPO attempts to bring about compliance through voluntary means, including any changes to the policies or practices of the institution. The penalty for noncompliance with FERPA can be withholding payments of Department of Education funds from the institution, issuing a cease and desist order, or terminating eligibility to receive funds; such actions generally will be taken only if compliance cannot be secured by voluntary means. *See* "Enforcement Procedures" (on page 92) for more information.

Conflict with State Law

FERPA may be more permissive than the privacy laws of some states. If a conflict exists between FERPA and a state or local law, and if an institution determines that it cannot comply with the requirements of The Act, it should advise the Student Privacy Policy Office, U.S. Department of Education, 400 Maryland Avenue, SW, Washington, D.C. 20202-5920; phone: (202) 260-

3887; email: <ferpa@ed.gov>, within 45 days of that determination, giving the text and legal citation of the conflicting law. These guidelines, therefore, should not be interpreted to reduce the stringency of such state laws. They counsel common sense, good judgment, perspective, and integrity for compliance by postsecondary institutions in the implementation of The Act.

Several challenges to FERPA were made during the 1990s based on various states' open records/meetings laws. In general, sunshine/open records laws do not supersede FERPA; thus, schools must continue to comply with FERPA. Any perceived conflict between a state open records law and FERPA should be brought to the attention of the Student Privacy Policy Office.

The "Musts" and "Mays" in FERPA

Throughout The Act, the words "may" and "must" are used. These words are usually used in connection with sections of The Act that either permit or require an institution to perform an action to comply with FERPA. In the former case, the institution has control over a decision; in other words, it *may* do something. In the latter case, the institution has no choice; in other words, it *must* do something.

There are many "mays" and a few "musts" in FERPA. The reader should be aware of these words and not consider an institution legally obliged to release education record information when FERPA actually states that the institution *may* release education record information. For example, FERPA states that each institution may identify certain items as directory information; however, this is an institutional decision. By deciding not to identify any items as directory information, the institution would be making a decision that could have a major administrative impact on all offices. For example, consider the challenges of producing a commencement program if the names of all the graduates and their degrees were not identified as directory information.

Note that the "may" under FERPA could become a "must" for public institutions in a state where the Open Records Law requires release of information that FERPA permits to be released, or under other legislation that might require all institutions in that state to release information releasable under FERPA.

CHAPTER TWO

FERPA At-A-Glance

If you are looking for a summary of what FERPA is all about, the following statements capture its essence:

- Students at postsecondary institutions must be permitted to inspect and review their education records.
- School officials may not disclose personally identifiable information from a student's education record, without written permission, unless such a disclosure is permitted by one of the FERPA signed-consent exceptions.
- Institutions are responsible for ensuring that all of its school officials comply with FERPA.

If you are looking for a more detailed summary of FERPA, the following will be helpful.

What is FERPA?

The *Family Educational Rights and Privacy Act of 1974*, as amended, sets forth requirements regarding the privacy of student records. This law applies to postsecondary institutions as well as K–12 schools.

FERPA governs:

- The disclosure of education records maintained by an educational institution; and
- Access to these records.

Who *must* comply with FERPA?

Any educational institution (school or other entity that provides educational services and is attended by students) or educational agency (entity that administers schools directly linked to it) that receive funds under any program administered by the U.S. Secretary of Education.

What does FERPA require for colleges to be in compliance?

- Institutions must notify students annually of their FERPA rights (*see* Appendix D, "Model Notification of Rights under FERPA for Postsecondary Institutions," on page 107).

  There is no specific method that schools must use to notify students—it is up to the institution. Notice must take a form that is "reasonably likely" to notify students. Recommended and most frequently used ways include: student bulletin, handbook or catalog; school or local newspaper; student registration packet; email notice of basic issues with a link to additional information.
- Ensure students' rights to inspect and review their education records.
- Ensure students' rights to request to amend their education records.
- Ensure students' rights to limit disclosure of personally identifiable information contained in education records.
- Notify third parties of the redisclosure prohibition of personally identifiable information (except under a few circumstances).
- Keep records of requests for and disclosures of student education records.

Who has FERPA rights at the postsecondary level?

- FERPA rights belong to the student at a postsecondary institution regardless of age.
- *Student* applies to all students—including continuing education students, students auditing a class, distance education students, and former students.
- *In attendance* can be defined by the institution, but it cannot be later than the day that the student first attends a class at the institution.

What FERPA rights are given to students?

- Right to inspect and review their education records.

- Right to request to amend their education records.
- Right to limit disclosure of "personally identifiable information" (information that would directly identify the student or make the student's identity easily traceable).
- Right to file a complaint with the Department of Education concerning an alleged failure by the institution to comply with FERPA.

What are education records under FERPA?

- Education records are defined as records that are:
  - Directly related to a student, and
  - Maintained by an educational agency or institution or by a party acting for the agency or institution.
- Education records are not: sole possession records, law enforcement unit records, employment records, medical records, or post-attendance records.

To whom, and under what conditions, can colleges disclose personally identifiable information?

- Anyone, if the college has obtained the prior written consent of the student
- Anyone, in response to requests for directory information (information that is generally not considered harmful or an invasion of privacy if disclosed)
  - Institutions must identify those items it considers directory information and notify students.
  - Institutions must inform students that they can withhold release of this information.
- Authorized representatives of the following government entities, if the disclosure is in connection with an audit or evaluation of federal or state supported education programs, or for the enforcement of or compliance with federal legal requirements that relate to those programs:
  - Comptroller General of the U.S.
  - Secretary of Education
  - U.S. Attorney General (for law enforcement purposes only)
  - State and local educational authorities

- School officials determined by the institution to have a legitimate educational interest
- Agents acting on behalf of the institution (*e.g.* contractors, consultants)
- Schools in which the student seeks or intends to enroll (additional conditions exist)
- A party, such as the Department of Veteran's Affairs or an employer, providing financial aid to the student ("financial aid" does not include any payments made by parents); (additional conditions exist)
- Organizations conducting studies for or on behalf of educational institutions (additional conditions exist)
- Accrediting organizations for accreditation purposes
- Parents of a dependent student (as defined by the IRS code)
- Parents when their student (under 21) is found to have violated the alcohol or drug policy of the institution
- To comply with a judicial order or subpoena, including *ex parte* orders under the USA Patriot Act
- Appropriate parties if a health or safety emergency exists and the information will assist in resolving the emergency (additional conditions exist)
- The student
- An alleged victim of a crime of violence when the disclosure is the results of a disciplinary hearing regarding the alleged perpetrator of that crime with respect to that crime
- Anyone requesting the final results of a disciplinary hearing against an alleged perpetrator who has been found in violation of the campus code relating to a crime of violence or non-forcible sex offense
- The Department of Homeland Security (DHS), Immigration and Customs Enforcement (ICE) for purpose of complying with Request Form ICE relative to the institution's participation in SEVIS
- Military recruiters who request "Student Recruiting Information" for recruiting purposes only (Solomon Amendment). Student recruiting information is name, address, telephone listing, age (or year of birth), class level, major, degrees received and most recent educational institution of enrollment. (conditions exist)
- The Internal Revenue Service (IRS), for purposes of complying with the *Taxpayer Relief Act of 1997*

- Anyone, when the disclosure concerns information provided by sex offenders required to register under state or federal law

How does technology impact FERPA guidelines?

As we move toward an environment with less paper, it is important to note that the same principles of access and confidentiality must be applied to all media, including but not limited to, electronic data, email, and video or audio tapes.

What happens if a college does *not* comply with FERPA?

The Department of Education may issue a notice to cease the non-compliance and could ultimately withhold funds administered by the Secretary of Education.

Where can I get more information regarding FERPA?

Student Privacy Policy Office
U.S. Department of Education
400 Maryland Avenue, SW
Washington, DC 20202–5920
Phone: (202) 260-3887
Email: <ferpa@ed.gov>
Web: <ed.gov/policy/gen/guid/fpco/>

Assistance is also available from AACRAO at <aacrao.org/ferpa> and <pubs@aacrao.org>.

CHAPTER THREE

Definition of Terms

Understanding key terms is essential to the interpretation of The Act and the final regulations for its implementation. Some definitions and explanations which carry substantive meaning for understanding The Act are listed here for the convenience of the reader. The regulations, as contained in Appendix A to this guide, provide all legal definitions.

ACT: Refers to the *Family Educational Rights and Privacy Act of 1974*, as amended, enacted as Section 444 of the *General Education Provisions Act* (20 U.S.C. 1232g).

AGENCY: An organization, company, or bureau that provides some service for another; a company having a franchise to represent another.

AGENT: A person or business formally authorized to act on another's behalf, *e.g.* within the scope of a contract between the two parties.

ALLEGED PERPETRATOR OF A CRIME OF VIOLENCE: A student who is alleged to have committed a crime of violence or a non-forcible sex offense.

ALUMNI RECORD: A record created by an educational institution that may contain personally identifiable information about a former student; is related solely to that student's activities as an alumnus; and is not related to attendance as a student.

ALUMNUS: A graduate or former student of a specific school, college, or university.

ATTENDANCE: Includes but is not limited to:

- Attendance in person or by paper correspondence, videoconference, satellite, internet, or other electronic information and telecommunications technologies for students who are not physically present in the classroom.
- The period during which a person is working in a work-study program.

AUTHORIZED REPRESENTATIVE: any entity or individual designated by a state or local educational authority or an agency headed by an official listed in 99.31(a)(3) to conduct—with respect to federal or state supported education programs—any audit, evaluation, or compliance or enforcement activity in connection with federal legal requirements that relate to these programs. This could include: state health and human services agencies, state labor agencies, and any other public or private entity.

BIOMETRIC RECORD: As used in the definition of "personally identifiable information," a record of one or more measurable biological or behavioral characteristics that can be used for automated recognition of an individual. Examples include fingerprints, retina and iris patterns, voiceprints, DNA sequence, facial characteristics, and handwriting.

CALIFORNIA CONSUMER PRIVACY ACT: Referred to in this publication as CCPA, is a state statute intended to enhance privacy rights and consumer protection for residents of California. The law, enacted in 2018 and effective January 1, 2020, creates new consumer rights relating to the access to, deletion of, and sharing of personal information that is collected by for-profit entities operating in the state.

C.F.R.: See "Code of Federal Regulations" on page 13.

CCPA: *See* "California Consumer Privacy Act."

CLERY ACT: The *Jeanne Clery Disclosure of Campus Security Policy and Campus Crime Statistics Act,* codified at 20 U.S.C. 1092 (f) as a part of the *Higher Education Act of 1965*, is a federal law that requires colleges and universities to disclose certain timely and annual information about campus crime and security policies. All public and private postsecondary educational institutions participating in federal student aid programs are subject to it. The Clery Act was originally enacted by Congress in 1990 as the Campus Security Act. It requires colleges and universities to publish an annual report every year by October 1 containing three years' worth of crime statistics and certain security policy statements, including sexual assault policies—which assure basic victims' rights—the law enforcement authority of campus police, and where the students should go to report crimes.

CODE OF FEDERAL REGULATIONS: The annual accumulation of executive agency regulations published in the daily Federal Register, combined with regulations issued previously and still in effect. The C.F.R. contains the general body of regulatory laws governing practice and procedure before federal administrative agencies. The regulations pertaining to FERPA are found in 34 C.F.R. Part 99 (*see* Appendix A, on page 55).

CONTRACTOR: Outside parties who, for the purposes of The Act, qualify as school officials in that they are acting for the agency or institution and are subject to the same conditions governing the access and use of records that apply to other school officials.

COURT ORDER: A directive issued by a Court of Law requiring an entity to take some specified action.

CRIME OF VIOLENCE: Refers to acts that would, if proven, constitute any of the following offenses or attempts to commit the following offenses: arson, assault, burglary, negligent homicide, criminal homicide, destruction/damage/vandalism of property, kidnapping/abduction, robbery, forcible sex offenses, non-forcible sex offenses.

DATES OF ATTENDANCE: The period of time during which a student attends or attended an institution. Examples of dates of attendance include an academic year, a spring semester, or a first quarter. The term does not include specific daily records or a student's attendance at the institution.

DE-IDENTIFIED RECORDS AND INFORMATION: An educational record that has had all personally identifiable information, as defined in §99.31(b), removed.

DIGITAL MILLENNIUM COPYRIGHT ACT, THE: The Recording Industry Association of America continues to issue subpoenas for names and addresses of students whose internet service provider address or internet names correlate to evidence of music sharing. In response to campus inquiries about whether or not to disclose an education record pursuant to a subpoena, the FPCO advises that institutions may do so *as long as a reasonable attempt is made* to give the student prior notice. The DMCA criminalizes a) the circumvention of technological measures that serve to protect copyrighted material, b) the manufacture or distribution of software whose specific purpose is to bypass or circumvent these digital protection measures, and c) the production or distribution of programs and software with altered or removed technological copyright protection systems without the consent or knowledge of the copyright owner. The Act can be viewed at <copyright.gov/legislation/pl105-304.pdf>.

DIRECTORY INFORMATION: Information contained in an education record of a student that would not generally be considered harmful or an invasion of privacy if disclosed. It includes, but is not limited to: the student's name, address, telephone listing, e-mail address, photograph, date and place of birth, major field of study, grade level, enrollment status (*e.g.*, undergraduate or graduate, full-time or part-time), dates of attendance, participation in officially recognized activities and sports; weight and height of members of athletic teams; degrees, honors and awards received; and the most recent educational agency or institution attended.

(a) Directory information does *not* include a student's—(1) Social security number; or (2) Student identification (ID) number, except as provided in paragraph (b) of this section.

(b) Directory information includes a student ID number, user ID, or other unique personal identifier used by the student for purposes of accessing or communicating in electronic systems, but only if the identifier cannot be used to gain access to education records except when used in conjunction with one or more factors that authenticate the user's identity, such as a personal identification number (PIN), password, or other factor known or possessed only by the authorized user.

NON-DISCLOSURE/OPT-OUT/NO RELEASE OF DIRECTORY INFORMATION: The requirement that an educational institution must provide the opportunity for a student to refuse to let the institution release information designated as Directory Information, as outlined in §99.37.

DISCIPLINARY ACTION OR PROCEEDING: The investigation, adjudication, or imposition of sanctions by an educational agency or institution with respect to an infraction or violation of the internal rules of conduct applicable to students of the agency or institution.

FINAL RESULTS OF A DISCIPLINARY PROCEEDING: A decision or determination, made by an honor court or council, committee, commission, or other entity authorized to resolve disciplinary matters within the institution. The disclosure of final results must include only the name of the student, the violation committed, and any sanction imposed by the institution against the student.

DISCLOSURE: To permit access to, or the release, transfer, or other communication of, personally identifiable information contained in education records by any means, including oral, written, or electronic means, to any party except the party identified as the party that provided or created the record.

EASILY TRACEABLE: This term was removed in the 2009 regulations and replaced with the language in §99.3, "personally identifiable information," (f) and (g).

ELECTRONIC SIGNATURE: An electronic sound, symbol, or process, attached to or logically associated with a contract or other record and executed or adopted by a person with the intent to sign the record that identifies and authenticates that person as the source of the electronic consent, and indicates such person's approval of the information contained in the electronic consent.

EDI: *See* "Electronic Data Interchange" on page 16.

EDUCATIONAL INSTITUTION: Generally refers to any public or private agency, institution (including governing boards which provide administrative control or direction of a university system) of postsecondary education, which receives funds from any federal program under the administrative responsibility of the Secretary of Education. The term refers to the institution as a whole, including all of its components (*e.g.*, schools or departments in a university).

EDUCATION PROGRAM: Any program that is principally engaged in the provision of education, including, but not limited to, early childhood education, elementary and secondary education, postsecondary education, special education, job training, career and technical education, adult education and any program that is administered by an educational agency or institution.

EDUCATION RECORDS: Those records directly related to a student and maintained by the institution or by a party acting for the institution.

Education records *do not* include:

(1) Records that are kept in the sole possession of the maker, are used only as a personal memory aid, and are not accessible or revealed to any other person except a temporary substitute for the maker of the record.

(2) Records of the law enforcement unit of an educational agency or institution, subject to the provisions of §99.8.

(3) Records relating to an individual who is employed by an educational agency or institution, that:

(A) are made and maintained in the normal course of business;

(B) relate exclusively to the individual in that individual's capacity as an employee; and

(C) are not available for use for any other purpose.

(N.B. Records relating to an individual in attendance at the agency or institution who is employed as a result of his or her status as a student are education records and not excepted under paragraph (b)(3)(i) [*see* page 42] of this definition.)

(4) Records on a student who is 18 years of age or older, or is attending an institution of postsecondary education, that are:

(i) made or maintained by a physician, psychiatrist, psychologist, or other recognized professional or paraprofessional acting in his or her professional capacity or assisting in a paraprofessional capacity;

(ii) made, maintained, or used only in connection with treatment of the student; and

(iii) disclosed only to individuals providing the treatment. For the purpose of this definition, "treatment" does not include remedial educational activities or activities that are part of the program of instruction at the agency or institution.

(5) Records created or received by an educational agency or institution after an individual is no longer a student in attendance and that are not directly related to the individual's attendance as a student.

(6) Grades on peer-graded papers before they are collected and recorded by a teacher.

ELECTRONIC DATA INTERCHANGE: Utilizes standard data formats for transmitting data from one computer to another.

ELIGIBLE STUDENT: Refers to a student who has reached the age of 18 *or* is attending an institution of postsecondary education. Since these guidelines are specifically for postsecondary institutions, "student" as used in this document is presumed always to refer to an eligible student. In non-postsecondary institutions, parents of students have additional rights not covered in this guide.

ENROLLED STUDENT: For the purposes of this publication, this term refers to a student who has satisfied all of the institutional requirements for attendance at the institution. The Department of Education has stated that each institution may determine when a student is "*in attendance*" in accordance with its own enrollment procedures. (*Federal Register*, July 6, 2000, p. 41856).

EX PARTE ORDER: An order issued by a court of competent jurisdiction without notice to an adverse party in connection with the investigation or prosecution of terrorism crimes specified in sections 2331 and 2332b(g)(5)(B) of Title 18, U.S. Code.

FAMILY POLICY COMPLIANCE OFFICE: Prior to 2017, this office (also known as the FPCO) was the office within the U.S. Department of Education responsible for enforcing/administering the *Family Educational Rights and Privacy Act of 1974* (FERPA) as amended.

FINANCIAL AID: A payment of funds to an individual (or a payment in kind of tangible or intangible property to the individual), which is conditioned on the individual's attendance at an educational agency or institution. Financial aid does not include payments made by parents.

GDPR: *See* "General Data Protection Regulation."

GENERAL DATA PROTECTION REGULATION: Referred to in this publication as GDPR, is a regulation adopted by the European Union (EU) in 2016 on the protection of natural persons with regard to the processing of personal data and on the free movement of such data. The regulation repealed and replaced the EU's Data Protection Directive of 1995 (Directive 95/46/EC). The GDPR, effective May 2018, represents a significant expansion of personal privacy rights for EU residents. It applies to all institutions involved in processing data about citizens in the EU, regardless of whether the organization is located within the EU. As such, the GDPR would almost certainly apply to all U.S. higher education institutions.

GRAMM-LEACH-BLILEY: The *Gramm-Leach-Bliley Act of 1999* prohibits an institution that provides financial products or services from sharing a customer's "nonpublic personal information" with non-affiliated third parties unless the institution first discloses its privacy policy to consumers and allows them to "opt out" of that disclosure. The Act restricts the ability to sell, give or otherwise disclose personal information to third parties without permission.

HEALTH AND SAFETY EMERGENCY: An educational agency or institution may disclose personally identifiable information from an education record to appropriate parties including parents of an eligible student, in connection with an emergency if knowledge of the information is necessary to protect the health or safety of the student or other individuals.

HIPAA: The *Health Insurance Portability and Accountability Act of 1996* requires the establishment of national standards for electronic health care transactions and national identifiers for providers, health insurance plans, and employers with the intention of keeping patient information private.

IN ATTENDANCE (OR WHEN IS A STUDENT "IN ATTENDANCE"?): *See* "Enrolled Student" on page 17 .

INSTITUTION OF POSTSECONDARY EDUCATION: An institution that provides education to students beyond the secondary school level. "Secondary school level" means the educational level (not beyond grade 12) at which secondary education is provided.

LAW ENFORCEMENT UNIT: Any individual or other component of an institution, including commissioned police officers and noncommissioned security guards, officially authorized by the institution to enforce any local, state, or federal law and maintain the physical security and safety of the institution. (Although the unit may perform other non-law enforcement functions, it retains its status as a law enforcement unit.)

LAW ENFORCEMENT UNIT RECORDS: These records are not education records as defined by The Act, so long as the records are files, documents, and other materials that are: 1) created by a law enforcement unit, 2) created for a law enforcement purpose, and 3) maintained by the law enforcement unit. Law enforcement records *do not* include: 1) records created by a law enforcement unit for law enforcement purposes other than those of the law enforcement unit; and 2) records created and maintained by a law enforcement unit exclusively for non–law enforcement purposes, such as a disciplinary action or proceeding conducted by the institution.

LEGITIMATE EDUCATIONAL INTEREST: The demonstrated "need to know" by those officials of an institution who act in students' educational interest, including faculty, administration, clerical and professional employees, and other persons who manage student record information including student employees or agents. (Although The Act does not define "legitimate educational interest," it states that institutions must establish their own criteria, according to their own procedures and requirements, for determining when their school officials have a legitimate educational interest in a student's education records.) *See* Appendix D, "Model Notification of Rights under FERPA for Postsecondary Institutions" (on page 107), which contains sample language.

MEGAN'S LAW: Established the minimum national standards for sex offender registration and community notification programs. States must establish programs that require a sexually violent predator (and anyone convicted of specified criminal offenses against minors) to register their name and address with the appropriate authority where the offender lives, works, or is enrolled as a student. States are also required to release relevant information necessary to protect the public concerning persons required to register, excluding the identity of any victim. Under FERPA, prior consent is not required if the disclosure concerns sex offenders under Section 170101 of the *Violent Crime Control and Law Enforcement Act of 1994*, 42 U.S.C. 14071 and the information was provided to the educational agency or institution under 42 U.S.C. 14071 and applicable federal guidelines.

NON-DISCLOSURE/OPT-OUT/NO RELEASE OF DIRECTORY INFORMATION: *See* "Directory Information" on page 14.

NON-FORCIBLE SEX OFFENSE: Statutory rape or incest.

OUTSOURCING: The circumstances under which a business contracts with another business to conduct a service or function that it would otherwise provide itself. In many cases the contracted business will be acting as an "agent" (*see also* "Agent" on page 11) of the contracting business.

PARENT: Includes a natural parent (custodial and/or non-custodial), a guardian, or an individual acting as a parent in the absence of a parent or a guardian.

PARTY: Refers to an individual, agency, institution, or organization.

PERSONALLY IDENTIFIABLE: Data or information which includes, but is not limited to (a) the student's name; (b) the name of the student's parent or other family members; (c) the address of the student or student's family; (d) a personal identifier, such as the student's social security number, student number, or biometric record; (e) other indirect identifiers, such as the student's date of birth, place of birth, and mother's maiden name; (f) other information that, alone or in combination, is linked or linkable to a specific student and that would allow a reasonable person in the school community who does not have personal knowledge of the relevant circumstances to identify the student with reasonable certainty; or (g) information requested by a person who the educational agency or institution reasonably believes knows the identity of the student to whom the education record relates.

RECORD: Any information or data recorded in any medium (*e.g.*, handwriting, print, tapes, film, microfilm, microfiche, database, any form of electronic data storage including emails).

RECORDKEEPING: Recordation of releases of personally identifiable information from a student's education records to a party outside of the institution. Includes health or safety emergency releases. *See* §99.32 of the FERPA regulations (on page 81) for more details, including exceptions.

REDISCLOSURE: Notification requirement for institutions of higher education and state educational authorities acting on behalf of the institution concerning the disclosure of personally identifiable information from education records to parties outside the institution. *See* §99.3 (on page 59) for details, including exceptions. In most instances under FERPA third parties are prohibited from redisclosing student education data.

REGULATIONS, THE: Federal regulations implementing the statutory requirements of FERPA and found in Appendix A (on page 55). Also cited in this publication as 34 C.F.R. Part 99. Throughout this *Guide*, we have eliminated the "C.F.R." symbol where possible and have substituted the section symbol (§) before the specific regulation discussed.

REVERSE TRANSFER: The transfer of credits from a four-year institution to a two-year institution from which a student transferred for the purpose of facilitating the awarding of an associate's degree or certificate.

SEVIS: The Student and Exchange Visitor Information System (SEVIS) is an internet-based system that establishes a process for electronic reporting by designated school officials of information required to be reported to the Department of Homeland Security's Immigration and Customs Enforcement (ICE), previously known as the Immigration and Naturalization Service (INS). SEVIS maintains accurate and current information on non-immigrant students (F and M visa), exchange visitors (J visa), and their dependents (F-2, M-2, and J-2). SEVIS enables schools and program sponsors to transmit mandatory information and event notifications via the internet, to ICE throughout a student's or exchange visitor's stay in the United States, in order to certify an institution as eligible to participate in SEVIS.

SCHOOL OFFICIALS: Those members of an institution who act in the student's educational interest within the limitations of their "need to know." These may include faculty, administration, clerical and professional employees and other persons who manage student education record information including student employees or agents. It may also include contractors, volunteers, and others performing institutional functions. (Although The Act does not define "school officials," it states that institutions must establish their own criteria, according to their own procedures and requirements for determining them. This is a recommended definition.)

SOLE POSSESSION RECORDS: Records that are kept in the sole possession of the maker, are used only as a personal memory aid, and are not accessible or revealed to any other person except a temporary substitute for the maker of the record. Sole possession records do not include records made in conjunction with a student or other school official, such as an evaluation of a student or the student's performance.

SOLOMON AMENDMENT: Sometimes referred to in this publication simply as "Solomon." This 1996 amendment requires postsecondary institutions to provide Department of Defense representatives, among other things, access to student recruiting information (defined below).

SPPO: *See* "Student Privacy Policy Office" on page 22.

STUDENT: Any individual for whom an educational institution maintains education records. The term "student" does not include an individual who has not been in attendance at the institution. An individual who is or has been enrolled in one component unit of an institution and applies for admission to a second unit has no right to inspect the records accumulated by the second unit until enrolled therein.

STUDENT PRIVACY POLICY OFFICE: The office within the U. S. Department of Education that is currently responsible for enforcing/administering the Family Educational Rights and Privacy Act of 1974 (FERPA) as amended. This office has responsibility for FERPA at all levels of education (K-12, postsecondary).

STUDENT RECRUITING INFORMATION: Information identified in the Solomon Amendment that institutions are required to provide military recruiters upon request. Those items are: student name, addresses, telephone listings, age or year of birth, class level, academic major, degrees received and the most recent previous educational institution in which the student was enrolled.

STUDENT RIGHT-TO-KNOW ACT OF 1990: Referred to in this publication as SRTK, it requires colleges and universities to report graduation rates to current and prospective students.

SUBPOENA: A command from a court to require the person named in the subpoena to appear at a stated time and place to provide testimony or evidence. There are two main types of subpoenas: *duces tecum* requires the production of documents, papers or other tangibles and ad *testificandum* requires a person to testify in a particular court case.

USA PATRIOT ACT: The *Uniting and Strengthening America by Providing Appropriate Tools Required to Intercept and Obstruct Terrorism (*USA PATRIOT*) Act of 2001* permits a postsecondary institution to disclose personally identifiable information from a student's education records—without notification of the student—to the U. S. Attorney General or his designee in order to comply with an *ex parte* order in connection with the investigation or prosecution of an offense listed in 18 U.S.C. 2332(g)(5)(B).

U.S.C.: United States Code. A compilation of all federal legislation organized into 50 titles. Revised every six years with supplementary volumes issued in intervening years. The legislation related to FERPA is found in 20 U.S.C. 1232g.

CHAPTER FOUR

FERPA Basics for Faculty and Instructors

The following document is intended to serve as a one-page, double-sided summary of FERPA, particularly focused toward faculty and instructional staff. It can be used as a handout as well as a training tool.

The Essence

- Federal law designed to protect the privacy of education records. It also provides guidelines for appropriately using and releasing student education records.
- It is intended that students' rights be broadly defined and applied. Therefore, consider the student as the "*owner*" of the information in their education record, and the institution as the "*custodian*" of that record.

Key Terms/Definitions

"EDUCATION RECORDS" include any record maintained by the institution that contains information that is personally identifiable to a student (in whatever format or medium) with some narrowly defined exceptions:

- Records in the "sole possession of the maker" (*e.g.*, private advising notes).
- Law enforcement records created and maintained by a law enforcement agency for a law enforcement purpose.

- Employment records (unless the employment is based on student status). The employment records of student employees (*e.g.*, work-study, wages, graduate teaching associates) are part of their education records.
- Medical/psychological treatment records (*e.g.*, from a health or counseling center).
- Alumni records (*i.e.*, those created after the student graduated or left the institution).

"DIRECTORY INFORMATION:" Those data items that are generally not considered harmful or an invasion of privacy if publicly available. This information cannot be released if student has a "no release" on their record. Each institution establishes what it considers to be directory information. Common examples include: name, address (local, home and email), telephone (local and home), academic program of study, dates of attendance, date of birth, most recent educational institution attended, and degrees and awards received.

- Directory information *cannot* include: race, gender, SSN (or part of an SSN), grades, GPA, country of citizenship, or religion. Except in very specific circumstances, a student ID number (SIN) also cannot be considered directory information.
- Every student must be given the opportunity to have directory information suppressed from public release. This process is often referred to as a "no release," "opt out" or "suppression." When a student makes this request, everyone within the institution must abide by a student's request that no information be released about the student.
- It is important to understand, that a "no release" does *not* mean that a school official within the institution who has a demonstrated legitimate educational interest (*e.g.*, a faculty member teaching the student in class) is precluded from using the information to perform that official's job duties.

"PARENT:" With reference to FERPA, the term "parent" refers to either parent (including custodial and non-custodial, if divorced).

When do FERPA rights begin?

A FERPA-related college education record begins for a student when he or she enrolls in a higher education institution. At a postsecondary institution, rights belong to the student in attendance, regardless of the student's age.

Basic Rights of Students under the Act

- Be notified of their FERPA rights at least annually.
- Inspect and review their records.
- Amend an incorrect record.
- Consent to disclosure (with exceptions).

ANNUAL NOTIFICATION

Every institution must notify students of their FERPA rights at least annually.

INSPECTION AND REVIEW

Students have the *right* to see everything in their "education record," except:

- Information about other students;
- Financial records of parents; and
- Confidential letters of recommendation if they waived their right of access.

FERPA does not prescribe what records are created or how long they are to be kept; however, you cannot destroy a record if there is a request to inspect and review. It is important to know and understand your institution's records retention policy.

RIGHT TO CONSENT TO DISCLOSURE

Start with the premise that the student has the right to control to whom their education record is released. Then, there are several exceptions when that permission is not required.

In those instances where a signed release is required, regulations now provide the flexibility to accept an electronic signature.

When is prior consent not required?

The institution may disclose records without consent if certain requirements are met, but it is not required to do so.

Some examples of the exceptions to the release requirement include:

- "School officials" with a "legitimate educational interest." Employees and legal agents have access to education records in order to perform their official, educationally-related duties.
- Disclosure to organizations conducting studies to improve instruction, or to accrediting organizations.
- Disclosure to parents of *dependent students* (IRS definition); check to see how your institution expects parents to demonstrate student dependent status.
- To comply with a judicial order or lawfully issued subpoena.
- Disclosure for a health/safety emergency (must document what the emergency was and to whom the information was released).
- Disclosure of directory information, provided the student has not requested "no release."

Specific Issues for Faculty and Instructional Staff

- **POSTING GRADES:** Since grades can never be directory information, it is inappropriate to post grades in a public setting. An instructor may, however, post grades if the grades are posted in such a manner that only the instructor and the individual student can identify the individual and their grade. Grades should never be posted by any portion of the SSN or student ID. Additionally, any posted list should not be in the same order as the class roster or in alphabetical order.
- **WEB-BASED TOOLS TO SUPPORT CLASSES:** Courses supported by class websites and/or discussion groups must take extra precautions to not inadvertently release non-directory student information. Only directory information can be available to the general public and other class members, so web-based tools should employ a security layer so that only class members and instructors can access appropriate information.

- **STUDENTS OPTING FOR NO RELEASE IN THE CLASSROOM SETTING:** Students cannot choose to be anonymous in the classroom setting. If a student has chosen "no release" for their directory information, that does not mean that an instructor cannot call on the student by name in class or that the student's email address cannot be displayed on an electronic classroom support tool such as a discussion board, blog, or chat feature.

CHAPTER FIVE

FERPA Basics for Administrative Staff

The following document is intended to serve as a one-page, double-sided summary of FERPA, particularly focused toward staff in an office that regularly works with student education records. It can be used as a handout as well as a training tool.

The Essence

- Federal law designed to protect the privacy of education records. It also provides guidelines for appropriately using and releasing student education records.
- It is intended that students' rights be broadly defined and applied. Therefore, consider the student as the "*owner*" of the information in their education record, and the institution as the "*custodian*" of that record.

Key Terms/Definitions

"EDUCATION RECORDS" include any record maintained by the institution that contains information that is personally identifiable to a student (in whatever format or medium) with some narrowly defined exceptions:

- Records in the "sole possession of the maker" (*e.g.*. private advising notes).
- Law enforcement records created and maintained by a law enforcement agency for a law enforcement purpose.

- Employment records (unless the employment is based on student status). The employment records of student employees (*e.g.*, work-study, wages, graduate teaching associates) are part of their education records.
- Medical/psychological treatment records (*e.g.*, from a health or counseling center).
- Alumni records (*i.e.*, those created after the student graduated or left the institution).

"DIRECTORY INFORMATION:" Those data items that are generally not considered harmful or an invasion of privacy if publicly available. Cannot be released if student has a "no release" on their record. Each institution establishes what it considers to be directory information. Common examples include: name, address (local, home and email), telephone (local and home), academic program of study, dates of attendance, date of birth, most recent educational institution attended, and degrees and awards received.

- Directory Information *cannot* include: race, gender, SSN (or part of an SSN), grades, GPA, country of citizenship, or religion. Except in very specific circumstances, a student ID number (SIN) also cannot be considered directory information.
- Every student must be given the opportunity to have directory information suppressed from public release. This process is often referred to as a "no release," "opt out" or "suppression." Everyone within the institution must abide by a student's request that no information be released about the student.
- It is important to understand, that a "no release" does *not* mean that a school official within the institution who has a demonstrated legitimate educational interest (*e.g.*, faculty member teaching the student in class) is precluded from using the information to perform that official's job duties.

"PARENT:" With reference to FERPA, the term "parent" refers to either parent (including custodial and non-custodial, if divorced).

When do FERPA rights begin?

A FERPA-related college education record begins for a student when he or she enrolls in a higher education institution. At a postsecondary institution, rights belong to the student in attendance, regardless of the student's age.

Basic Rights of Students under the Act:

- Be notified of their FERPA rights at least annually.
- Inspect and review their records.
- Amend an incorrect record.
- Consent to disclosure (with exceptions).

ANNUAL NOTIFICATION

Every institution must notify students of their FERPA rights at least annually.

INSPECTION AND REVIEW

Students have the *right* to see everything in their "education record," except:

- Information about other students.
- Financial records of parents.
- Confidential letters of recommendation if they waived their right of access.

FERPA does not prescribe what records are created or how long they are to be kept; however, you cannot destroy a record once there is a request to inspect and review. It is important to know and understand your institution's records retention policy.

RIGHT TO CONSENT TO DISCLOSURE

Start with the premise that the student has the right to control to whom their education record is released. Then, there are several exceptions when that permission is not required.

In those instances where a signed release is required, regulations now provide the flexibility to accept an electronic signature.

When is prior consent not required?

The institution may disclose records without consent if certain requirements are met, but it is not required to do so. Some examples of the exceptions to the release requirement include:

- "School officials" with a "legitimate educational interest." Employees and legal agents have access to education records in order to perform their official, educationally-related duties.
- Disclosure to another institution where the student seeks to enroll or is enrolled.
- Disclosure to DOE, state/local education authorities.
- Disclosure in connection with the receipt of financial aid.
- Disclosure to state/local officials in conjunction with legislative requirements.
- Disclosure to organizations conducting studies to improve instruction, or to accrediting organizations.
- Disclosure to parents of *dependent students* (IRS definition). Check to see how your institution expects parents to demonstrate student dependent status.
- To comply with a judicial order or lawfully issued subpoena.
- Disclosure for a health/safety emergency (must document what the emergency was and to whom the information was released).
- Disclosure of directory information provided the student has not requested "no release."
- Disciplinary information:
  - Disclosure to the alleged victim of a crime of violence, such as information from disciplinary proceedings.
  - *Only* when found in violation, and *only* for crimes of violence—release of name, sanction and outcome can be made to anyone.
- Disclosure to parents of any student under the age of 21, a violation of federal, state, local or institutional laws/regulations related to substance abuse (provided that other laws governing the institution, such as state law, do not preclude such disclosures).

FERPA rights at a postsecondary institution end with a student's death. However, state law may provide for a continued right to privacy in your state. Students have a formal right to file a complaint with the Department of Education.

Checklist for Requests for Access to or Disclosure of Information from Education Records

- Is the information in question an education record under FERPA?
- Is the information personally identifiable?
- Is the information considered directory information?
    - Is the subject of the request a current student, or a graduate/student no longer in attendance?
    - Did the student request a directory hold when he/she had the opportunity to do so?
    - Do you need to comply with the request?
- Does the disclosure require signed consent?
    - Does the disclosure meet one of the exceptions to signed consent found in §99.31 of FERPA?
    - Is the disclosure required to supplement other information, such as financial aid information?
- Do you have a State open records law that directs you to treat information differently, but in a way still permitted by FERPA?

Key Resources for Additional Information:

- Your campus registrar
- AACRAO (Compliance)—<aacrao.org/ferpa/>
- Student Privacy Policy Office of the Department of Education (administers FERPA compliance)—<ed.gov/policy/gen/guid/fpco/>

CHAPTER SIX

General Data Protection Regulation (GDPR) and State Privacy Laws

In April 2016, the European Parliament adopted the General Data Protection Regulation (GDPR), which specifies how consumer data of citizens in the European Union (EU) should be used and protected. The regulation repealed and replaced the EU's Data Protection Directive of 1995 (Directive 95/46/EC).

The GDPR, effective May 2018, represents a significant expansion of personal privacy rights for EU residents. The new law resulted from the need to protect data and privacy rights of individuals as highly sensitive personal information of EU students, employees, and others become increasingly digitized. It applies to all institutions involved in processing data about citizens in the EU, regardless of whether the organization is located within the EU. As such, the GDPR would almost certainly apply to all U.S. higher education institutions.

While compliance and interpretation of the GDPR are legal issues and its provisions are complex, the regulation provides an opportunity for higher education to engage in a process to identify and review data flows, processing, and management, as well as a chance to update policies and procedures.

The GDPR differs greatly from American privacy laws in scope and specific parameters. The regulation broadly defines personal data as any information relating to an identified or identifiable natural person ("data subject")—including educational, financial, employment-related, and health data, but also photographs, personal phone numbers, and IP addresses. It subjects all personally identifiable data to its core requirements and provides additional protections for "sensitive personal data" that include racial and ethnic origin, religion, sexual orientation, and political views, among other things. Under the regulation, the processing of personal data is generally prohibited unless certain requirements are satisfied.

Under United States privacy laws and regulations, in contrast, the processing of personal information is generally permitted. American privacy laws and regulations also take a more patchwork approach, addressing privacy and data practices by sector (*e.g.*, FERPA, HIPAA, state data breach notification laws). Each sectoral law or regulation define specific data elements as personal information.

Many GDPR provisions are reflected in the United States' requirements on the use of data in certain instances and in certain sectors. For example, the concepts related to the GDPR "Right of Rectification," which gives individuals the right to have personal data rectified if it is inaccurate or incomplete, are similar to those outlined in FERPA. However, the EU's requirements are more comprehensive, universal, and not limited to certain data elements or industry sectors. Additionally, some provisions in the GDPR are somewhat novel. The "Right to be Forgotten," which includes a data subject's right to erasure of data, halt in dissemination of data, and potentially halting third party processing of data, is the provision that seems to provoke the most concern among higher education administrators.

What is the General Data Protection Regulation (GDPR)?

The following information on GDPR is adapted from the Implications of the General Data Protection Regulation: An Interassociation Guide. The document is the collaborative result from a wide array of professional education associations, including AACRAO. For the full guide and the most recent information on GDPR, visit <aacrao.org/advocacy/compliance/gdpr>.

For an overview of frequently asked GDPR questions, *see* Appendix F, "GDPR FAQ" (on page 119).

The subject matter and the objectives of the GDPR, as laid out in Article 1 states:

- This Regulation lays down rules relating to the protection of natural persons with regard to the processing of personal data and rules relating to the free movement of personal data.

- This Regulation protects fundamental rights and freedoms of natural persons and in particular their right to the protection of personal data.
- The free movement of personal data within the EU shall be neither restricted nor prohibited for reasons connected with the protection of natural persons with regard to the processing of personal data.

In more specific terms, the Territorial Scope is outlined in Article 3:

- This Regulation applies to the processing of personal data in the context of the activities of an establishment of a controller or a processor in the EU, regardless of whether the processing takes place in the EU or not.
- This Regulation applies to the processing of personal data of data subjects who are in the EU by a controller or processor not established in the EU, where the processing activities are related to:
  - the offering of goods or services, irrespective of whether a payment of the data subject is required, to such data subjects in the EU; or
  - the monitoring of their behavior as far as their behavior takes place within the EU.
- This Regulation applies to the processing of personal data by a controller not established in the EU, but in a place where Member State law applies by virtue of public international law.

The GDPR outlines the requirements necessary for data handling, maintenance, and retention, collectively referred to as "processing." In order to comply with GDPR, institutions need to consider creating practices based on these requirements. (*See* Table 1, on page 38.)

Comparing GDPR and FERPA

Institutional compliance with FERPA is insufficient for complying with GDPR. Fundamentally, the scope and specific parameters are quite different. While FERPA protects student records at American colleges and universities, its requirements fall short of the broad reach of the GDPR. (*See* Table 2, on page 39.)

Table 1

Section	Article(s)	Processing Order
Transparency	12	Individuals should be provided with notice on what personal data is being processed and the purposes for that processing.
Consent	7	Should be clear and distinguishable.
Breach Notification	33, 34	Mandatory and within 72 hours.
Data Minimization	5, 25	Personal data shall be adequate, relevant and limited to what is necessary in relation to the purposes for which they are processed.
Right to Access	15	Controller obliged to confirm and provide access to and copy of data (free of charge).
Right of Rectification	16	The GDPR gives individuals the right to have personal data rectified if it is inaccurate or incomplete.
Right to be Forgotten (Right to Erasure)	17	There are conditions, but this does include right to erasure of data, halt in dissemination of data, and potentially halting third party processing of data.
Data Portability	20	Gives data subject right to obtain data in commonly used and machine readable format, and the right to transmit that data to another controller.
Privacy by Design	25	Meaning data protection at all stages and throughout a system. This may require a formal "certification" that processing platforms meet privacy requirements.
Data Protection Officers	37, 38, 39	Appointment of Data Protection Officers (DPOs) is intended to make adherence and compliance local and accountable. GDPR outlines several items to ensure the DPO is equipped and supported in carrying out duties.

State Privacy Laws

In the wake of the European Union's General Data Protection Regulation (GDPR), a growing number of states across America are considering comprehensive privacy legislation of their own. New laws in California and Nevada are the first of these to take effect.

CALIFORNIA CONSUMER PRIVACY ACT (CCPA)

The California Consumer Privacy Act (CCPA), enacted in 2018 and effective January 1, 2020, creates new consumer rights relating to the access to, deletion of, and sharing of personal information that is collected by businesses. It is the most comprehensive state privacy measure to date in the United States

Table 2

	FERPA	GDPR
Purpose	The Family Educational Rights and Privacy Act of 1974, as amended, sets forth requirements regarding the privacy of student records.	To enable the free movement of personal data within the EU while protecting fundamental rights and freedoms of natural persons and, in particular, their right to the protection of personal data.
Material Scope	FERPA applies to K-12 schools and postsecondary institutions. Specifically for this match-up, the scope is limited to Eligible Students (those 18 or those attending an institution of higher education regardless of age).	Applies to the processing of personal data wholly or partly by automated means, within the scope of EU law.
Territorial Scope	Any educational institution (school or other entity that provides educational services and is attended by students) or educational agency (entity that administers schools directly linked to it) that receive funds under any program administered by the U.S. Secretary of Education.	Applies to processing that takes place in the Union or by a processor who has an establishment in the EU within the context of activities in the EU or to processing activities that are related to the offering of goods and services to (or behavioral monitoring of) data subjects in the EU.
Personal Data	Personally Identifiable Information—(Information that would directly identify the student or make the student's identity easily traceable) known as directory information. Educational Records—directly related to a student and maintained by an educational agency or institution or by a party acting for the agency or institution.	Personal data means any information relating to an identified or identifiable natural person (the "data subject"). An identifiable natural person is anyone that can be identified, either directly or indirectly, by reference to anything that can ultimately identify them. This includes a name, an identification number, location data, an online identifier or to data that relates to the physical, physiological, genetic, mental, economic, cultural or social identity of that natural person.
Sensitive Personal Data	In the 2009 regulations clarification was provided that a social security number (SSN), or part of an SSN, cannot be designated as directory information. In addition, the revised regulations apply this restriction to Student Identification Numbers (SIN).* Grades, GPA, race, gender, religion and national origin are also items that cannot be designated as directory information.	Special categories of data that are considered particularly sensitive are personal data revealing racial or ethnic origin, political opinions, religious or philosophical beliefs, or trade union membership, and the processing of genetic data, biometric data for the purpose of uniquely identifying a natural person, data concerning health or data concerning a natural person's sex life or sexual orientation.

* **Exception:** "A student ID number, user ID, or other unique personal identifier used by the student for purposes of accessing or communicating in electronic systems" can be directory information "only if the identifier cannot be used to gain access to education records without an additional factor" (AACRAO 2012).

and serves as a template for numerous other state proposals. The law protects the personal data of "residents" of California—either by living in California or temporarily outside the state—collected by any company that does business in California for profit.

CCPA applies to any business that:

- has annual gross revenue of more than 25 million,
- buys, receives, sells, or shares the personal information of 50,000+ "residents," or
- derives more than 50 percent of their annual revenue from the sale of personal data.

Personal data subject to HIPAA and certain other laws are exempted from the CCPA, but data subject to FERPA are not included in those exemptions.

Most significantly, according to a 2020 AACRAO Connect article, a for-profit institution of higher education that qualifies as a "business" under the CCPA must, among other obligations:

- at or before the collection of personal information, inform consumers of the categories of personal information to be collected and the purpose for which personal information will be used;
- make disclosures in its privacy policy about its consumer personal information, the sources of the personal information, the purposes for collecting or selling the personal information, the categories of third parties to whom it shares the personal information, and that a consumer has a right to request their personal information from the business;
- disclose that the consumer has the right to request deletion of their personal information (although there are several exceptions regarding which data are subject to this deletion requirement);
- upon a consumer's request, provide the consumer with the consumer's personal information, as well as certain information about the personal information (*e.g.* its source and purpose) and about its disclosure or sale; and
- if the business sells consumer personal information (under a broad definition of "sell"), provide notice to consumers that their personal information may be sold, offer them a right to opt-out of such sales, and respect a consumer's exercise of their opt-out right.

The CCPA also applies in various ways to service providers and other third parties that receive consumer personal information from businesses. (Locklin 2020)

NEVADA PRIVACY OF INFORMATION COLLECTED ON THE INTERNET FROM CONSUMERS ACT

The Nevada Privacy of Information Collected on the Internet from Consumers Act (NPICICA) was amended in June 2019 through Nevada Senate Bill 220 to include a requirement to allow consumers to opt-out of certain data disclosures.

The amended law, effective October 1, 2019, applies only to operators who:

- own or operate an Internet website or online service for commercial purposes,
- collect and maintain covered information from Nevada residents who use or visit the Internet website or online service, and
- engage in any activity that constitutes a sufficient nexus with Nevada.

Personal data subject to HIPAA and certain other laws are exempted, but data subject to FERPA are not included in those exemptions.

Enacted Laws

	California	Nevada
Right of Access	X	
Right of Rectification		
Right of Deletion	X	
Right of Restriction		
Right of Portability	X	
Right of Opt-Out	X	X
Notice/Transparency Requirement	X	X
Data Breach Notification		X

Proposed Legislation

Since the enactment of the GDPR and the CCPA, lawmakers in at least twenty-four states have unveiled legislative proposals to regulate personal consumer data privacy. Other states are likely to follow suit. Most of the state proposals aim to give residents new rights to ownership over their data and establish new transparency requirements for entities that process personal data. Individuals would have the right to access, delete, correct, and move their data, or opt-out of data collection. Although many of the measures will fail to become law, state-level momentum for comprehensive privacy bills appears to be on the rise.

On the federal level, lawmakers have also proposed legislation that would create an overarching, federal data-privacy framework, as opposed to a patchwork of confusing state laws. The measures are generally consistent with the current data-privacy legal frameworks and integrate themes from the CCPA and the European Union's GDPR. Thus far, most would exempt personal data subject to FERPA, HIPAA, and certain other laws. The likelihood of passage of federal comprehensive privacy legislation is narrow at this time. However, the need to protect data and privacy rights of individuals as personal data becomes increasingly digitized remains.

CHAPTER SEVEN

Remote Work and Virtual Learning during Emergencies

The COVID-19 pandemic forced higher education to navigate through uncommon territory to protect the health and safety of institutions and students. Institutions moved quickly to establish new practices and policy exceptions around their actions to move courses and services online or to other remote delivery. The shift to virtual learning and remote work during the national emergency presented unprecedented challenges, drastically changing campus environments and daily operations. It also prompted school officials to reevaluate how their institutions comply with the *Family Educational Rights and Privacy Act* (FERPA) when adopting remote work and distance learning approaches.

This chapter highlights updated guidance from the Department of Education and best practices on student privacy, health and safety considerations, virtual access of student records, and other implications for remote work and virtual learning.

Health or Safety Emergency

Postsecondary officials are regularly asked to balance the interests of safety and privacy for individual students. FERPA typically does not allow institutions to disclose information about students without their consent, including details about their health. However, in the case of a health or safety emergency, such as the COVID-19 pandemic, FERPA permits school officials to disclose without student consent education records, including personally identifiable information (PII) from those records, to protect the health or safety of students or other individuals. At such times, records and information may be released to appropriate parties such as law enforcement officials, public health officials, and trained medical personnel. *See* 34 C.F.R. 99.31 (a) (10) and 99.36. This exception to FERPA's general consent rule is limited to the period of the emergency and generally does not allow for a blanket release of personally identifiable information from a student's education records. In addition, the Department interprets FERPA to permit institutions to disclose information from education records to parents if a health or safety emergency involves their child.

The Student Privacy Policy Office recently provided updated guidance to assist school officials in protecting student privacy in the context of COVID-19 as they consider the disclosure of PII from student education records to individuals and entities who may not already have access to that information. Additional information and more detailed guidance on FERPA is available on SPPO's website at <studentprivacy.ed.gov>.

QUESTIONS FOR CONSIDERATION[1]

Do eligible students have to provide consent before an educational institution discloses PII from education records?

Generally, yes. An eligible student must provide written consent before an institution discloses PII from a student's education records, unless one of the exceptions to FERPA's general consent rule applies. *See* 34 C.F.R. 99.30 and 99.31.

How does the health or safety emergency exception to FERPA's consent requirement permit an institution to disclose PII from the education records of affected students?

Although institutions can often address threats to the health or safety of students or other individuals in a manner that does not identify a particular student, FERPA permits institutions to disclose, without prior written consent, PII from student education records to appropriate parties in connection with an emergency, if knowledge of that information is necessary to protect

[1] AACRAO has edited this guidance to emphasize the postsecondary items and also supplemented certain discussions.

the health or safety of a student or other individuals. *See* 34 C.F.R. 99.31(a)(10) and 99.36.

May student education records, such as health records, maintained by an institution be disclosed, without consent, to public health departments if the educational institution believes that the virus that causes COVID-19 poses a serious risk to the health or safety of an individual student in attendance at the educational agency or institution?

Yes. If an educational institution, taking into account the totality of the circumstances, determines that an articulable and significant threat exists to the health or safety of a student in attendance at the institution (or another individual at the institution) as a result of the virus that causes COVID-19, it may disclose, without prior written consent, PII from student education records to appropriate officials at a public health department who need the information to protect the health or safety of the student (or another individual).

Does an interagency agreement with partners such as the State or local health department enable a school to nonconsensually disclose education records?

No. Interagency agreements do not supersede the consent requirements under FERPA. Although an interagency agreement would be a helpful tool for planning purposes, schools must comply with FERPA's requirements regarding the disclosure of personally identifiable information from students' education records.

If an educational institution learns that student(s) in attendance at the school are out sick due to COVID-19, may it disclose information about the student's illness under FERPA to other students in the school community without prior written consent of the student?

It depends, but generally yes, but generally only if that information is in a non-personally identifiable form. Specifically, the educational institution must make a reasonable determination that a student's identity is not personally identifiable, whether through single or multiple releases, and taking into account other reasonably available information. *See* 34 C.F.R. 99.31(b)(1).

FERPA does permit school officials to disclose, without consent, education records, or personally identifiable information from education records, to appropriate parties in connection with an emergency, if knowledge of that information is necessary to protect the health or safety of the student or other individuals. *See* 34 C.F.R. 99.31(a)(10), 99.32(a)(5), and 99.36. This exception to FERPA's general consent requirement is temporally limited to the period of the emergency and generally does not allow for a blanket release of personally identifiable information from the student's education records. Typically, law enforcement officials, public health officials, trained medical personnel, and parents (including parents of an eligible student) are the types of appropriate parties to whom information may be disclosed under this FERPA exception.

Under this health or safety emergency provision, an institution is responsible for making a determination whether to make a disclosure of personally identifiable information on a case-by-case basis, taking into account the totality of the circumstances pertaining to the threat. If the school district or school determines that there is an articulable and significant threat to the health or safety of the student or other individuals and that certain parties need personally identifiable information from education records to protect the health or safety of the student or other individuals, it may disclose that information to such appropriate parties without consent. 34 C.F.R. 99.36. This is a flexible standard under which the Department defers to school administrators so that they may bring appropriate resources to bear on the situation, provided that there is a rational basis for the institution's decisions about the nature of the emergency and the appropriate parties to whom information should be disclosed. We note also that, within a reasonable period of time after a disclosure is made under this exception, an institution must record in the student's education records the articulable and significant threat that formed the basis for the disclosure and the parties to whom information was disclosed. 34 C.F.R. 99.32(a)(5). Oftentimes, however, threats to health or safety can be fully addressed by sharing appropriate information regarding such threats with parents, the health department, or others in a manner that does not identify particular students.

Under FERPA, an emergency means a situation in which there is an articulable and significant threat to the health or safety of students or other individuals. Note that an emergency can exist without a public health authority designation of an emergency. However, if public health authorities determine that a pandemic, such as COVID-19, is a significant threat to a particular community, a school in that community may determine that an emergency exists as well. As used in FERPA's health or safety emergency provision, an emergency does not include the threat of a possible or eventual emergency for which the likelihood of occurrence is unknown, such as would be addressed in general emergency preparedness activities. Accordingly, when disclosures are limited temporally to the period of the emergency, institutions may release information at any stage of such emergency so long as there is an articulable and significant threat in the community that may be addressed by the limited release of information to appropriate parties. This includes sharing information where necessary during the early stages of a pandemic.

May institutions disclose without consent the names, addresses, and phone numbers of absent students to the public health department so that the health department may contact their parents in order to assess the students' illnesses?

FERPA permits institutions to non-consensually disclose PII from education records in the form of contact information of absent students to the public health department in specific circumstances, such as in connection with a health or safety emergency (34 C.F.R. 99.31(a)(10) and 99.36) or pursuant to other applicable exceptions.

If an institution determines that a health or safety emergency exists, may it disclose, without consent, PII from student education records to the media?

No. FERPA only permits nonconsensual disclosures of PII from students' education records under the health or safety emergency exception to "appropriate parties" (such as public health officials) whose knowledge of the information is necessary to protect the health or safety of students or other individuals.

May the school identify a particular student, a teacher, or other school official as having COVID-19 to parents of other students in the school?

In most cases, it is sufficient to report the fact that an individual in the school has been determined to have COVID-19, rather than specifically identifying the student who is infected. In some instances, however, it may be deemed appropriate to identify the student.

May an educational institution disclose PII from an eligible student's education records to the student's parents if the eligible student has been determined to have COVID-19?

Yes, for dependent students and generally yes, but see below. Under FERPA, an educational institution, including an institution of postsecondary education, may disclose, without the eligible student's written consent, PII from an eligible student's education records to their parents under certain conditions. For example, a university physician treating an eligible student for COVID-19 might determine that the student's treatment records should be disclosed to the student's parents. This disclosure may be made, without consent of the eligible student, if the parents claim the eligible student as a dependent under section 152 of the Internal Revenue Code of 1986. *See* 34 C.F.R. 99.31(a)(8). If the parents do not claim the eligible student as a dependent, then the disclosure may be made to the parents, without the eligible student's written consent, if the disclosure is in connection with a health or safety emergency provided certain conditions are satisfied. *See* 34 C.F.R. 99.31(a)(10) and 99.36.

Is an educational institution required to record disclosures of PII from student education records submitted to the public health department or other outside parties, even in connection with a health or safety emergency?

Yes. FERPA generally requires educational institutions to maintain a record of each request for access to and each disclosure of PII from the education records of each student. See 34 C.F.R. 99.32(a)(1). Moreover, when making a disclosure under the health or safety emergency provision in FERPA, educational institutions are specifically required to record the articulable and significant threat to the health or safety of a student or other individual that formed the basis for the disclosure and the parties to whom the institution disclosed the information. *See* 34 C.F.R. 99.32(a)(5).

For additional advice on the disclosure of personally identifiable information to various emergency situations on campus, *see* Appendix E, "FPCO/SPPO Guidance Brochure for Colleges" (on page 113), *see also* Appendix F, "Addressing Emergencies on Campus" in the *AACRAO 2012 FERPA Guide.*

Remote Work

The move to remote work, due to campus closures or otherwise, presents a number of challenges with regard to FERPA compliance, including email communications with student information, right to access records, electronic consent, and the use of third-party vendors or service providers, among other things. The following information provides privacy best practices and other resources for schools officials to ensure that institutions continue to adhere to FERPA under changing work environments.

SCHOOL OFFICIAL EXCEPTION TO THE GENERAL CONSENT REQUIREMENT

FERPA does not prohibit school officials from taking PII from students' education records to their remote working environments, provided that the school official has a legitimate educational interest in the education records, as determined by their institution. School officials, including instructors, are prohibited from further disclosing the PII from the education records, except as otherwise permitted under FERPA; and, should use reasonable methods to protect the education records held in remote working environments from further disclosure.

Additional Considerations

- Protections can include access controls that are physical, technological, and administrative.
- If using a personal device to access your student information system (SIS) when not on campus, make sure there is a Virtual Private Network (VPN) installed. Consult your institution's Information Technology department to inquire about any additional security steps you can take to minimize the risk of hacks or other theft of PII that can occur when using personal devices.

EMAIL AND STUDENT PRIVACY

An essential component of remote work is the ability to connect and communicate. In an increasingly digital world, email is one of the most common forms of communication on campus. As institutions move to working remotely, the ability to communicate and operate virtually is critical. Prior to sending an email, it is important that school officials evaluate the risk associated with sending student information and recognizing if it is PII.

Best Practices on How to Email Student Information—

- Consider what information is included in the email prior to sending. Even a combination of seemingly non-identifiable information could allow someone in the campus community to identify the student.
- If the email includes FERPA-protected PII, weigh the risks and benefits of sending such information electronically to reduce the chance of inadvertent disclosure of student PII.
- Review institutional policies regarding emailing PII and follow those requirements. Consider encrypting documents or other data containing student PII, even if the policy does not require encryption, or consider using Secure File Transfer Protocol (SFTP).
- Use strong passwords.
- Include sensitive information in a protected file attachment, not in the body of the email.
- Do not include more information than necessary.
- Double-check the recipient's email address, especially for bulk emails and carbon copied recipients.
- Double-check the file attachment to ensure it is the intended document.

Specific Issues for Faculty and Instructional Staff—

- Emailing grades: Grades can never be directory information, under FERPA. Therefore, instructors communicating with students using email should follow the best practices on emailing student information when discussing grades.
- Cellular phone communication: The best practice is to communicate with students solely through institutional email accounts. However, FERPA does not prohibit the use of cellular phone or text communication between an instructor and a student. The key is that it must be with the student. To ensure that the exchange meets the requirements set forth in 34 C.F.R. 99.30, obtain the prior written consent of the student to permit phone calls or texting to a listed cell phone number.

RIGHT TO ACCESS RECORDS

Institutional closures complicated the process of complying with some of students' basic privacy rights under FERPA. However, certain steps must still be taken to ensure access to education records. Under FERPA, institutions must comply with an eligible student's request for access to the student's education records within 45 days of the receipt of a request. While required to provide access to education records, institutions are not generally required under FERPA to provide copies of education records.

However, if circumstances effectively prevent the eligible student from exercising the right to inspect and review the student's education records, the institution is required to either provide a copy of the records requested or make other arrangements for the eligible student to inspect and review the requested records.

ELECTRONIC CONSENT[2]

FERPA permits electronic consent. A "signed and dated written consent" under FERPA may include a record and signature in electronic form that:

- Identifies and authenticates a particular person as the source of the electronic consent; and
- Indicates such person's approval of the information contained in the electronic consent.

Additional Considerations—

- Specify the records that may be disclosed.
- State the purpose of the disclosure
- Identify the party or class of parties to whom the disclosure may be made.
- Request additional information to authenticate the identity of the individual if an email is not already on file.

THIRD-PARTY VENDORS OR SERVICE PROVIDERS

In order to ease the transition to remote work, institutions may look to third-party vendors and service providers as they move services online or to other remote delivery options. While FERPA is technology neutral, any vendor used by an institution would need to ensure that no improper disclosure of education records results. The Act provides a set of legal requirements that

[2] For federal guidelines for accepting signed and dated written consent in electric format, as well as safe harbor requirements, *see* Appendix J, "Electronic Signature Regulations," in the *2012 AACRAO FERPA Guide*.

protect education records contained within the hosted systems regardless of who maintains them, but it is the institution's responsibility to provide the explicit terms of service.

At a minimum, vendor contracts should include terms relating to the ownership of the data being stored, the status of deleted information, how data will be protected, and limitations of the use of data. For additional information, *see* Appendix G, "FERPA Guidance for Contracts and Written Agreements" (on page 123).

VIRTUAL LEARNING

Distance education and online educational services have grown increasingly popular in recent years. The COVID-19 pandemic, however, forced many institutions to unexpectedly and rapidly transition to online learning. The following information provides best practices and other resources for schools officials to ensure that institutions continue to adhere to FERPA when using online educational services.

Under the school official exception to FERPA's general consent requirement, institutions may disclose students' education records, or PII in those records, to a provider of such a service or application as long as the provider:

- Performs an institutional service or function for which the institution would otherwise use its own employees.
- Has been determined to meet the criteria set forth in in the institution's annual notification of FERPA rights for being a school official with a legitimate educational interest in the education records or PII.
- Is under the direct control of the institution regarding the use and maintenance of the education records or PII.
- Uses the education records or PII only for authorized purposes and does not redisclose the education records or PII to other parties (unless the provider has specific authorization from the institution to do so and it is otherwise permitted by FERPA). *See* 34 C.F.R. 99.31(a)(1)(i).

For guidance concerning contracting terms and language as you seek to establish direct control of a service provider, *see* Appendix G, "FERPA Guidance for Contracts and Written Agreements," on page 123.

Best Practices for Protecting Student Privacy When Using Online Educational Services

When using online educational services, it is important to:

- Maintain awareness of other relevant federal, state, tribal, or local laws.
- Be aware of all online educational services being used at your institution.
- Have policies and procedures to evaluate and approve proposed online educational services.
- Use a written contract or legal agreement with any service provider.
- Take extra precautions when consumer applications require the acceptance of terms of service. A vendor's terms of service cannot require a student to accept them in order to receive a service.
- Be transparent.
- Determine whether consent is necessary.

Additional Considerations—

- At a minimum, contracts or written agreements should include terms relating to the ownership of the data being stored, the status of deleted information, how data will be protected, and limitations of the use of data. *See* Appendix G, "FERPA Guidance for Contracts and Written Agreements" (on page 123) for additional information.
- FERPA is a privacy rule and does not include explicit information security standards. It does however, require that the security standards used protect the student's education records from improper disclosure or use. Institutions should work with their information security officers and attorneys to review information security requirements and terms of service.

Specific Issues for Faculty and Instructional Staff—

- **POSTING GRADES:** Since grades can never be directory information, it is inappropriate to post grades in a public online forum. An instructor may, however, post grades if the grades are posted in such a manner that only the instructor and the individual student can identify the student's grade. Grades should never be posted by any portion of the

SSN or student ID. Additionally, such a posted list should not be in the same order as the class roster or in alphabetical order.

- **WEB-BASED TOOLS TO SUPPORT CLASSES:** Courses supported by class websites and/or discussion groups must take extra precautions to not inadvertently release non-directory student information. Only directory information can be available to the general public and other class members, thus it is important that such web-based tools employ a security layer so that only class members and instructors can access appropriate information.
- **STUDENTS OPTING FOR NO RELEASE IN THE CLASSROOM SETTING:** Students cannot choose to be anonymous in the classroom setting. If a student has chosen "no release" for their directory information, that does not mean that an instructor cannot call on the student by name in class or that the student's email address cannot be displayed on an electronic classroom support tool such as a discussion board, blog, or chat feature.
- **LECTURE CAPTURE VIDEOS:** FERPA does not prohibit instructors from making a recording of virtual lectures or class sessions available to students enrolled in the course. However, sharing the recordings beyond students enrolled in the course would generally require prior written consent.

Where can I get more information regarding FERPA Guidance on Remote Work and Virtual Learning?

Student Privacy Policy Office
U.S. Department of Education
400 Maryland Avenue, SW
Washington, D.C. 20202–5920
Phone: (202) 260-3887
Email: <ferpa@ed.gov>
Web: <studentprivacy.ed.gov>

APPENDIX A

Family Educational Rights and Privacy Act Regulations

Amendments have been highlighted for the convenience of readers. Changes made to the Act in 2009 are underlined while those made in 2012 are given a light grey background, as shown.

The Family Policy Compliance Office (or its predecessor in name) has overseen the implementation of FERPA since the enactment of the law in 1974. Historically, institutions have worked only with this office on all issues related to FERPA compliance and enforcement. However, the Obama administration issued a new rule in January 2017 changing the office that administers FERPA-related issues to the Student Privacy Policy Office. References to the Family Policy Compliance Office have been left intact in this Appendix to reflect the exact language of the Family Education Rights and Privacy Act.

34 C.F.R. Part 99

Subpart A—General

Section

99.1 To which educational agencies or institutions do these regulations apply?

99.2 What is the purpose of these regulations?

99.3 What definitions apply to these regulations?
99.4 What are the rights of parents?
99.5 What are the rights of students?
99.7 What must an educational agency or institution include in its annual notification?
99.8 What provisions apply to records of a law enforcement unit?

Subpart B—What Are the Rights of Inspection and Review of Education Records?

Section

99.10 What rights exist for a parent or eligible student to inspect and review education records?
99.11 May an educational agency or institution charge a fee for copies of education records?
99.12 What limitations exist on the right to inspect and review records?

Subpart C—What Are the Procedures for Amending Educating Records?

Section

99.20 How can a parent or eligible student request amendment of the student's education records?
99.21 Under what conditions does a parent or eligible student have the right to a hearing?
99.22 What minimum requirements exist for the conduct of a hearing?

Subpart D—May an Educational Agency or Institution Disclose Personally Identifiable Information from Education Records?

Section

99.30 Under what conditions is prior consent required to disclose information?
99.31 Under what conditions is prior consent not required to disclose information?
99.32 What recordkeeping requirements exist concerning requests and disclosures?

99.33 What limitations apply to the redisclosure of information?
99.34 What conditions apply to disclosure of information to other educational agencies or institutions?
99.35 What conditions apply to disclosure of information for federal or state program purposes?
99.36 What conditions apply to disclosure of information in health and safety emergencies?
99.37 What conditions apply to disclosing directory information?
99.38 What conditions apply to disclosure of information as permitted by state statute adopted after November 19, 1974 concerning the juvenile justice system?
99.39 What definitions apply to the nonconsensual disclosure of records by postsecondary educational institutions in connection with disciplinary proceedings concerning crimes of violence or non-forcible sex offenses?

Subpart E—What Are the Enforcement Procedures?

Section

99.60 What functions has the Secretary delegated to the Office and to the Office of Administrative Law Judges?
99.61 What responsibility does an educational agency or institution have concerning conflict with state or local laws?
99.62 What information must an educational agency or institution submit to the Office?
99.63 Where are complaints filed?
99.64 What is the investigation procedure?
99.65 What is the content of the notice of investigation issued by the Office?
99.66 What are the responsibilities of the Office in the enforcement process?
99.67 How does the Secretary enforce decisions?

Appendix A To Part 99—Crimes of Violence Definitions

Subpart A—General

§ 99.1 TO WHICH EDUCATIONAL AGENCIES OR INSTITUTIONS DO THESE REGULATIONS APPLY?

(a) Except as otherwise noted in § 99.10, this part applies to an educational agency or institution to which funds have been made available under any program administered by the Secretary, if—

(1) The education institution provides educational services or instruction, or both, to students; or

(2) The educational agency is authorized to direct and control public elementary or secondary, or postsecondary educational institutions.

(b) This part does not apply to an educational agency or institution solely because students attending that agency or institution receive non-monetary benefits under a program referenced in paragraph (a) of this section, if no funds under that program are made available to the agency or institution.

(c) The Secretary considers funds to be made available to an educational agency or institution if funds under one or more of the programs referenced in paragraph (a) of this section—

(1) Are provided to the agency or institution by grant, cooperative agreement, contract, subgrant, or subcontract; or

(2) Are provided to students attending the agency or institution and the funds may be paid to the agency or institution by those students for educational purposes, such as under the Pell Grant Program and the Guaranteed Student Loan Program (Titles IV-A-1 and IV-B, respectively, of the *Higher Education Act of 1965*, as amended).

(d) If an educational agency or institution receives funds under one or more of the programs covered by this section, the regulations in this part apply to the recipient as a whole, including each of its components (such as a department within a university).

[Authority: 20 U.S.C. 1232g]

§ 99.2 WHAT IS THE PURPOSE OF THESE REGULATIONS?

The purpose of this part is to set out requirements for the protection of privacy of parents and students under section 444 of the *General Education Provisions Act*, as amended.

[Authority: 20 U.S.C. 1232g]

Note to 99.2 "34 C.F.R. 300.610 through 300.626 contains requirements regarding the confidentiality of information relating to children with disabilities who receive evaluations, services or other benefits under Part B of the Individuals with Disabilities Education Act (IDEA). 34 C.F.R. 303.402 and 303.460 identify the confidentiality of information requirements regarding children and infants and toddlers with disabilities and their families who receive evaluations, services, or other benefits under Part C of IDEA. 34 C.F.R. 300.610 through 300.627 contain the confidentiality of information requirements that apply to personally identifiable data, information, and records collected or maintained pursuant to Part B of the IDEA."

§ 99.3 WHAT DEFINITIONS APPLY TO THESE REGULATIONS?

The following definitions apply to this part:

"ACT" means the *Family Educational Rights and Privacy Act of 1974*, as amended, enacted as section 444 of the *General Education Provisions Act.*

[Authority: 20 U.S.C. 1232g]

"ATTENDANCE" includes, but is not limited to:

(a) Attendance in person or by paper correspondence, videoconference, satellite, Internet, or other electronic information and telecommunications technologies for students who are not physically present in the classroom; and

(b) The period during which a person is working under a work-study program.

[Authority: 20 U.S.C. 1232g]

"AUTHORIZED REPRESENTATIVE" means any entity or individual designated by a State or local educational authority or an agency headed by an official listed in §99.31(a)(3) to conduct—with respect to Federal- or State-supported education programs—any audit or evaluation, or any compliance or enforcement activity in connection with Federal legal requirements that relate to these programs.

[Authority: 20 U.S.C. 1232g(b)(1)(C), (b)(3), and (b)(5)]

"BIOMETRIC RECORD," as used in the definition of "personally identifiable information," means a record of one or more measurable biological or behavioral characteristics that can be used for automated recognition of an individual. Examples include fingerprints; retina and iris patterns; voiceprints; DNA sequence; facial characteristics; and handwriting.

[Authority: 20 U.S.C. 1232g]

"DATES OF ATTENDANCE." (a) The term means the period of time during which a student attends or attended an educational agency or institution. Examples of dates of attendance include an academic year, a spring semester, or a first quarter.

(b) The term does not include specific daily records of a student's attendance at an educational agency or institution.

[Authority: 20 U.S.C. 1232g(a)(5)(A)]

"DIRECTORY INFORMATION" means information contained in an education record of a student that would not generally be considered harmful or an invasion of privacy if disclosed.

(a) Directory information includes, but is not limited to, the student's name, address, telephone listing, electronic mail address, photograph, date and place of birth, major field of study, dates of attendance, grade level, enrollment status (*e.g.*, undergraduate or graduate; full-time or part-time), participation in officially recognized activities and sports, weight and height of members of athletic teams, degrees, honors and awards received, and the most recent educational agency or institution attended.

(b) Directory information does not include a student's:

(1) Social security number; or

(2) Student identification (ID) number, except as provided in paragraph (c) of this definition.

(c) In accordance with paragraphs (a) and (b) of this definition, directory information includes—

(1) A student ID number, user ID, or other unique personal identifier used by a student for purposes of accessing or communicating in electronic systems, but only if the identifier cannot be used to gain access to education records except when used in conjunction with one or more factors that authenticate the user's identity, such as a personal identification number (PIN), password or other factor known or possessed only by the authorized user; and

(2) A student ID number or other unique personal identifier that is displayed on a student ID badge, but only if the identifier cannot be used to gain access to education records except when used in conjunction with one or more factors that authenticate the user's identity, such as a PIN, password, or other factor known or possessed only by the authorized user.

[Authority: 20 U.S.C. 1232g(a)(5)(A)]

"DISCIPLINARY ACTION OR PROCEEDING" means the investigation, adjudication, or imposition of sanctions by an educational agency or institution with respect to an infraction or violation of the internal rules of conduct applicable to students of the agency or institution.

"DISCLOSURE" means to permit access to or the release, transfer, or other communication of personally identifiable information contained in education records to any party, by any means, including oral, written, or electronic means. Disclosure means to permit access to or the release, transfer, or other communication of personally identifiable information contained in education records by any m eans, including oral, written, or electronic means, to any party except the party identified as the party that provided or created the record.

[Authority: 20 U.S.C. 1232g(b)(1) and (b)(2)]

"EARLY CHILDHOOD EDUCATION PROGRAM" means—

(a) A Head Start program or an Early Head Start program carried out under the Head Start Act (42 U.S.C. 9831 et seq.), including a migrant or seasonal Head Start program, an Indian Head Start program, or a Head Start program or an Early Head Start program that also receives State funding;

(b) A State licensed or regulated child care program; or

(c) A program that—

(1) Serves children from birth through age six that addresses the children's cognitive (including language, early literacy, and early mathematics), social, emotional, and physical development; and

(2) Is—

(i) A State prekindergarten program;

(ii) A program authorized under section 619 or part C of the Individuals with Disabilities Education Act; or

(iii) A program operated by a local educational agency.

"EDUCATION PROGRAM" means any program that is principally engaged in the provision of education, including, but not limited to, early childhood education, elementary and secondary education, postsecondary education, special education, job training, career and technical education, and adult education, and any program that is administered by an educational agency or institution.

(Authority: 20 U.S.C. 1232g(b)(3), (b)(5))

"EDUCATIONAL AGENCY OR INSTITUTION" means any public or private agency or institution to which this part applies under § 99.1(a).

[Authority: 20 U.S.C. 1232g(a)(3)]

"EDUCATION RECORDS" (a) The term means those records that are:

(1) Directly related to a student; and

(2) Maintained by an educational agency or institution or by a party acting for the agency or institution.

(b) The term does not include:

(1) Records that are kept in the sole possession of the maker, are used only as a personal memory aid, and are not accessible or revealed to any other person except a temporary substitute for the maker of the record.

(2) Records of the law enforcement unit of an educational agency or institution, subject to the provisions of § 99.8.

(3)(i) Records relating to an individual who is employed by an educational agency or institution, that:

(A) Are made and maintained in the normal course of business;

(B) Relate exclusively to the individual in that individual's capacity as an employee; and

(C) Are not available for use for any other purpose.

(ii) Records relating to an individual in attendance at the agency or institution who is employed as a result of his or her status as a student are education records and not excepted under paragraph (b)(3)(i) of this definition.

(4) Records on a student who is 18 years of age or older, or is attending an institution of postsecondary education, that are:

(i) Made or maintained by a physician, psychiatrist, psychologist, or other recognized professional or paraprofessional acting in his or her professional capacity or assisting in a paraprofessional capacity;

(ii) Made, maintained, or used only in connection with treatment of the student; and

(iii) Disclosed only to individuals providing the treatment. For the purpose of this definition, "treatment" does not include remedial educational activities or activities that are part of the program of instruction at the agency or institution; and

(5) Records created or received by an educational agency or institution after an individual is no longer a student in attendance and that are not directly related to the individual's attendance as a student.

(6) Grades on peer-graded papers before they are collected and recorded by a teacher.

[Authority: 20 U.S.C. 1232g(a)(4)]

"ELIGIBLE STUDENT" means a student who has reached 18 years of age or is attending an institution of postsecondary education.

[Authority: 20 U.S.C. 1232g(d)]

"INSTITUTION OF POSTSECONDARY EDUCATION" means an institution that provides education to students beyond the secondary school level; "secondary school level" means the educational level (not beyond grade 12) at which secondary education is provided as determined under state law.

[Authority: 20 U.S.C. 1232g(d)]

"PARENT" means a parent of a student and includes a natural parent, a guardian, or an individual acting as a parent in the absence of a parent or a guardian.

[Authority: 20 U.S.C. 1232g]

"PARTY" means an individual, agency, institution, or organization.

[Authority: 20 U.S.C. 1232g(b)(4)(A)]

"PERSONALLY IDENTIFIABLE INFORMATION" includes, but is not limited to:

(a) The student's name;
(b) The name of the student's parent or other family members;
(c) The address of the student or student's family;
(d) A personal identifier, such as the student's social security number or student number, or biometric record;
(e) Other indirect identifiers, such as the student's date of birth, place of birth, and mother's maiden name;
(f) Other information that, alone or in combination, is linked or linkable to a specific student that would allow a reasonable person in the school community, who does not have personal knowledge of the relevant circumstances, to identify the student with reasonable certainty; or
(g) Information requested by a person who the educational agency or institution reasonably believes knows the identity of the student to whom the education record relates.

[Authority: 20 U.S.C. 1232g]

"RECORD" means any information recorded in any way, including, but not limited to, handwriting, print, computer media, video or audio tape, film, microfilm, and microfiche.

[Authority: 20 U.S.C. 1232g]

"SECRETARY" means the Secretary of the U.S. Department of Education or an official or employee of the Department of Education acting for the Secretary under a delegation of authority.

[Authority: 20 U.S.C. 1232g]

"STUDENT," except as otherwise specifically provided in this part, means any individual who is or has been in attendance at an educational agency or institution and regarding whom the agency or institution maintains education records.

[Authority: 20 U.S.C. 1232g(a)(6)]

§ 99.4 WHAT ARE THE RIGHTS OF PARENTS?

An educational agency or institution shall give full rights under the *Act* to either parent, unless the agency or institution has been provided with evidence that there is a court order, state statute, or legally binding document relating to such matters as divorce, separation, or custody that specifically revokes these rights.

[Authority: 20 U.S.C. 1232g]

§ 99.5 WHAT ARE THE RIGHTS OF STUDENTS?

(a)(1) When a student becomes an eligible student, the rights accorded to, and consent required of, parents under this part transfer from the parents to the student.

(2) Nothing in this section prevents an educational agency or institution from disclosing education records, or personally identifiable information from education records, to a parent without the prior written consent of an eligible student if the disclosure meets the conditions in §99.31(a)(8), §99.31(a)(10), §99.31(a)(15), or any other provision in §99.31(a).

(b) The *Act* and this part do not prevent educational agencies or institutions from giving students rights in addition to those given to parents.

(c) An individual who is or has been a student at an education institution and who applies for admission at another component of that institution does not have rights under this part with respect to records maintained by that other component, including records maintained in connection with the student's application for admission, unless the student is accepted and attends that other component of the institution.

[Authority: 20 U.S.C. 1232g(d)]

§ 99.7 WHAT MUST AN EDUCATIONAL AGENCY OR INSTITUTION INCLUDE IN ITS ANNUAL NOTIFICATION?

(a)(1) Each educational agency or institution shall annually notify parents of students currently in attendance, or eligible students currently in attendance, of their rights under the *Act* and this part.

(2) The notice must inform parents or eligible students that they have the right to—

(i) Inspect and review the student's education records;

(ii) Seek amendment of the student's education records that the parent or eligible student believes to be inaccurate, misleading, or otherwise in violation of the student's privacy rights;

(iii) Consent to disclosures of personally identifiable information contained in the student's education records, except to the extent that the *Act* and § 99.31 authorize disclosure without consent; and

(iv) File with the Department a complaint under § 99.63 and § 99.64 concerning alleged failures by the educational agency or institution to comply with the requirements of the act and this part.

(3) The notice must include all of the following:

(i) The procedure for exercising the right to inspect and review education records.

(ii) The procedure for requesting amendment of records under § 99.20.

(iii) If the educational agency or institution has a policy of disclosing education records under § 99.31(a)(1), a specification of criteria for determining who constitutes a school official and what constitutes a legitimate educational interest.

(b) An educational agency or institution may provide this notice by any means that are reasonably likely to inform the parents or eligible students of their rights.

(1) An educational agency or institution shall effectively notify parents or eligible students who are disabled.
(2) An agency or institution of elementary or secondary education shall effectively notify parents who have a primary or home language other than English.

(Approved by the Office of Management and Budget under control number 1880–0508)

[Authority 20 U.S.C. 1232g(e) and (f)]

§ 99.8 WHAT PROVISIONS APPLY TO RECORDS OF A LAW ENFORCEMENT UNIT?

(a)(1) "Law enforcement unit" means any individual, office, department, division, or other component of an educational agency or institution, such as a unit of commissioned police officers or non-commissioned security guards, that is officially authorized or designated by that agency or institution to—

(i) Enforce any local, state, or federal law, or refer to appropriate authorities a matter for enforcement of any local, state, or federal law against any individual or organization other than the agency or institution itself; or
(ii) Maintain the physical security and safety of the agency or institution.

(2) A component of an educational agency or institution does not lose its status as a "law enforcement unit" if it also performs other, non-law enforcement functions for the agency or institution, including investigation of incidents or conduct that constitutes or leads to a disciplinary action or proceedings against the student.

(b)(1) Records of law enforcement unit means those records, files, documents, and other materials that are—

(i) Created by a law enforcement unit;
(ii) Created for a law enforcement purpose; and
(iii) Maintained by the law enforcement unit.

(2) Records of law enforcement unit does not mean—

(i) Records created by a law enforcement unit for a law enforcement purpose that are maintained by a component of the educational agency or institution other than the law enforcement unit; or
(ii) Records created and maintained by a law enforcement unit exclusively for a non-law enforcement purpose, such as a disciplinary action or proceeding conducted by the educational agency or institution.

(c)(1) Nothing in the *Act* prohibits an educational agency or institution from contacting its law enforcement unit, orally or in writing, for the purpose of asking that unit to investigate a possible violation of, or to enforce, any local, state, or federal law.

(2) Education records, and personally identifiable information contained in education records, do not lose their status as education records and remain subject to the *Act*, including the disclosure provisions of § 99.30, while in possession of the law enforcement unit.

(d) The *Act* neither requires nor prohibits the dis-closure by any educational agency or institution of its law enforcement unit records.

[Authority: 20 U.S.C. 1232g(a)(4)(B)(ii)]

Subpart B—What Are the Rights of Inspection and Review of Education Records?

§ 99.10 WHAT RIGHTS EXIST FOR A PARENT OR ELIGIBLE STUDENT TO INSPECT AND REVIEW EDUCATION RECORDS?

(a) Except as limited under § 99.12, a parent or eligible student must be given the opportunity to inspect and review the student's education records.

This provision applies to—

(1) Any educational agency or institution; and
(2) Any state educational agency (SEA) and its components.

(i) For the purposes of subpart B of this part, an SEA and its components constitute an educational agency or institution.

(ii) An SEA and its components are subject to subpart B of this part if the SEA maintains education records on students who are or have been in attendance at any school of an educational agency or institution subject to the *Act* and this part.

(b) The educational agency or institution, or SEA or its component, shall comply with a request for access to records within a reasonable period of time, but not more than 45 days after it has received the request.

(c) The educational agency or institution, or SEA or its component, shall respond to reasonable requests for explanations and interpretations of the records.

(d) If circumstances effectively prevent the parent or eligible student from exercising the right to inspect and review the student's education records, the educational agency or institution, or SEA or its component, shall—

(1) Provide the parent or eligible student with a copy of the records requested; or

(2) Make other arrangements for the parent or eligible student to inspect and review the requested records.

(e) The educational agency or institution, or SEA or its component, shall not destroy any education records if there is an outstanding request to inspect and review the records under this section.

(f) While an education agency or institution is not required to give an eligible student access to treatment records under paragraph (b)(4) of the definition of "Education records" in § 99.3, the student may have those records reviewed by a physician or other appropriate professional of the student's choice.

[Authority: 20 U.S.C. 1232g(a)(1)(A) and (B)]

§ 99.11 MAY AN EDUCATIONAL AGENCY OR INSTITUTION CHARGE A FEE FOR COPIES OF EDUCATION RECORDS?

(a) Unless the imposition of a fee effectively prevents a parent or eligible student from exercising the right to inspect and review the student's education records, an educational agency or institution may charge a fee for a copy of an education record which is made for the parent or eligible student.

(b) An educational agency or institution may not charge a fee to search for or to retrieve the education records of a student.

[Authority: 20 U.S.C. 1232g(a)(1)]

§ 99.12 WHAT LIMITATIONS EXIST ON THE RIGHT TO INSPECT AND REVIEW RECORDS?

(a) If the education records of a student contain information on more than one student, the parent or eligible student may inspect and review or be informed of only the specific information about that student.

(b) A postsecondary institution does not have to permit a student to inspect and review education records that are:

(1) Financial records, including any information those records contain, of his or her parents;

(2) Confidential letters and confidential statements of recommendation placed in the education records of the student before January 1, 1975, as long as the statements are used only for the purposes for which they were specifically intended; and

(3) Confidential letters and confidential statements of recommendation placed in the student's education records after January 1, 1975, if:

(i) The student has waived his or her right to inspect and review those letters and statements; and

(ii) Those letters and statements are related to the student's:

(A) Admission to an education institution;

(B) Application for employment; or

(C) Receipt of an honor or honorary recognition.

(c)(1) A waiver under paragraph (b)(3)(i) of this section is valid only if:

(i) The educational agency or institution does not require the waiver as a condition for admission to or receipt of a service or benefit from the agency or institution; and

(ii) The waiver is made in writing and signed by the student, regardless of age.

(2) If a student has waived his or her rights under paragraph (b)(3)(i) of this section, the education institution shall:

(i) Give the student, on request, the names of the individuals who provided the letters and statements of recommendation; and

(ii) Use the letters and statements of recommendation only for the purpose for which they were intended.

(3)(i) A waiver under paragraph (b)(3)(i) of this section may be revoked with respect to any actions occurring after the revocation.

(ii) A revocation under paragraph (c)(3)(i) of this section must be in writing.

[Authority: 20 U.S.C. 1232g(a)(1)(A), (B), (C), and (D)]

Subpart C—What Are the Procedures for Amending Education Records?

§ 99.20 HOW CAN A PARENT OR ELIGIBLE STUDENT REQUEST AMENDMENT OF THE STUDENT'S EDUCATION RECORDS?

(a) If a parent or eligible student believes the education records relating to the student contain information that is inaccurate, misleading, or in violation of the student's rights of privacy, he or she may ask the educational agency or institution to amend the record.

(b) The educational agency or institution shall decide whether to amend the record as requested within a reasonable time after the agency or institution receives the request.

(c) If the educational agency or institution decides not to amend the record as requested, it shall inform the parent or eligible student of its decision and of his or her right to a hearing under § 99.21.

[Authority: 20 U.S.C. 1232g(a)(2)]

§ 99.21 UNDER WHAT CONDITIONS DOES A PARENT OR ELIGIBLE STUDENT HAVE THE RIGHT TO A HEARING?

(a) An educational agency or institution shall give a parent or eligible student, on request, an opportunity for a hearing to challenge the content of the student's education records on the grounds that the information contained in the education records is inaccurate, misleading, or in violation of the privacy rights of the student.

(b)(1) If, as a result of the hearing, the educational agency or institution decides that the information is inaccurate, misleading, or otherwise in violation of the privacy rights of the student, it shall:

(i) Amend the record accordingly; and
(ii) Inform the parent or eligible student of the amendment in writing.

(2) If, as a result of the hearing, the educational agency or institution decides that the information in the education record is not inaccurate, misleading, or otherwise in violation of the privacy rights of the student, it shall inform the parent or eligible student of the right to place a statement in the record commenting on the contested information in the record or stating why he or she disagrees with the decision of the agency or institution, or both.

(c) If an educational agency or institution places a statement in the education records of a student under paragraph (b)(2) of this section, the agency or institution shall:

(1) Maintain the statement with the contested part of the record for as long as the record is maintained; and
(2) Disclose the statement whenever it discloses the portion of the record to which the statement relates.

[Authority: 20 U.S.C. 1232g(a)(2)]

§ 99.22 WHAT MINIMUM REQUIREMENTS EXIST FOR THE CONDUCT OF A HEARING?

The hearing required by § 99.21 must meet, at a minimum, the following requirements:

(a) The educational agency or institution shall hold the hearing within a reasonable time after it has received the request for the hearing from the parent or eligible student.

(b) The educational agency or institution shall give the parent or eligible student notice of the date, time, and place, reasonably in advance of the hearing.

(c) The hearing may be conducted by any individual, including an official of the educational agency or institution, who does not have a direct interest in the outcome of the hearing.
(d) The educational agency or institution shall give the parent or eligible student a full and fair opportunity to present evidence relevant to the issues raised under § 99.21. The parent or eligible student may, at their own expense, be assisted or represented by one or more individuals of his or her own choice, including an attorney.
(e) The educational agency or institution shall make its decision in writing within a reasonable period of time after the hearing.
(f) The decision must be based solely on the evidence presented at the hearing, and must include a summary of the evidence and the reasons for the decision.

[Authority: 20 U.S.C. 1232g(a)(2)]

Subpart D—May an Educational Agency or Institution Disclose Personally Identifiable Information from Education Records?

§ 99.30 UNDER WHAT CONDITIONS IS PRIOR CONSENT REQUIRED TO DISCLOSE INFORMATION?

(a) The parent or eligible student shall provide a signed and dated written consent before an educational agency or institution discloses personally identifiable information from the student's education records, except as provided in § 99.31.

(b) The written consent must:

(1) Specify the records that may be disclosed;
(2) State the purpose of the disclosure; and
(3) Identify the party or class of parties to whom the disclosure may be made.

(c) When a disclosure is made under paragraph (a) of this section:

(1) If a parent or eligible student so requests, the educational agency or institution shall provide him or her with a copy of the records disclosed; and

(2) If the parent of a student who is not an eligible student so requests, the agency or institution shall provide the student with a copy of the records disclosed.

(d) "Signed and dated written consent" under this part may include a record and signature in electronic form that—

(1) Identifies and authenticates a particular person as the source of the electronic consent; and

(2) Indicates such person's approval of the information contained in the electronic consent.

[Authority: 20 U.S.C. 1232g(b)(1) and (b)(2)(A)]

§ 99.31 UNDER WHAT CONDITIONS IS PRIOR CONSENT NOT REQUIRED TO DISCLOSE INFORMATION?

(a) An educational agency or institution may disclose personally identifiable information from an education record of a student without the consent required by § 99.30 if the disclosure meets one or more of the following conditions:

(1)(i)(A) The disclosure is to other school officials, including teachers, within the agency or institution whom the agency or institution has determined to have legitimate educational interests.

(B) A contractor, consultant, volunteer, or other party to whom an agency or institution has outsourced institutional services or functions may be considered a school official under this paragraph provided that the outside party—

(1) Performs an institutional service or function for which the agency or institution would otherwise use employees;

(2) Is under the direct control of the agency or institution with respect to the use and maintenance of education records; and

(3) Is subject to the requirements of §99.33(a) governing the use and redisclosure of personally identifiable information from education records.

(ii) An educational agency or institution must use reasonable methods to ensure that school officials obtain access to only those education records in which they have legitimate educational interests. An educational agency or institution that does not use physical or technological access controls must ensure that its administrative policy for controlling access to education records is effective and that it remains in compliance with the legitimate educational interest requirement in paragraph (a)(1)(i)(A) of this section.

(2) The disclosure is, subject to the requirements of § 99.34, to officials of another school, school system, or institution of postsecondary education where the student seeks or intends to enroll, or where the student is already enrolled so long as the disclosure is for purposes related to the student's enrollment or transfer.

Note: Section 4155(b) of the No Child Left Behind Act of 2001, 20 U.S.C. 7165(b), requires each State to assure the Secretary of Education that it has a procedure in place to facilitate the transfer of disciplinary records with respect to a suspension or expulsion of a student by a local educational agency to any private or public elementary or secondary school in which the student is subsequently enrolled or seeks, intends, or is instructed to enroll.

(3) The disclosure is, subject to the requirements of § 99.35, to authorized representatives of—

(i) The Comptroller General of the United States;
(ii) The Attorney General of the United States;
(iii) The Secretary; or
(iv) State and local educational authorities.

(4)(i) The disclosure is in connection with financial aid for which the student has applied or which the student has received, if the information is necessary for such purposes as to:

(A) Determine eligibility for the aid;
(B) Determine the amount of the aid;
(C) Determine the conditions for the aid; or
(D) Enforce the terms and conditions of the aid.

(ii) As used in paragraph (a)(4)(i) of this section, "financial aid" means a payment of funds provided to an individual (or a payment in kind of tangible or intangible property to the individual) that is conditioned on the individual's attendance at an educational agency or institution.

[Authority: 20 U.S.C. 1232g(b)(1)(D)]

(5)(i) The disclosure is to state and local officials or authorities to whom this information is specifically-

(A) Allowed to be reported or disclosed pursuant to a state statute adopted before November 19, 1974, if the allowed reporting or disclosure concerns the juvenile justice system and the system's ability to effectively serve the student whose records are released;or

(B) Allowed to be reported or disclosed pursuant to a state statute adopted after November 19, 1974, subject to the requirements of § 99.38.

(ii) Paragraph (a)(5)(1) of this section does not prevent a state from further limiting the number or type of state or local officials to whom disclosures may be made under that paragraph.

(6)(i) The disclosure is to organizations conducting studies for, or on behalf of, educational agencies or institutions to:

(A) Develop, validate, or administer predictive tests;

(B) Administer student aid programs; or

(C) Improve instruction.

(ii) Nothing in the Act or this part prevents a State or local educational authority or agency headed by an official listed in paragraph (a)(3) of this section from entering into agreements with organizations conducting studies under paragraph (a)(6)(i) of this section and redisclosing personally identifiable information from education records on behalf of educational agencies and institutions that disclosed the information to the State or local educational authority or agency headed by an official listed in paragraph (a)(3) of this section in accordance with the requirements of §99.33(b).

(iii) An educational agency or institution may disclose personally identifiable information under paragraph (a)(6)(i) of this section, and a State or local educational authority or agency headed by an official listed in paragraph (a)(3) of this section may redisclose personally identifiable information under paragraph (a)(6)(i) and (a)(6)(ii) of this section, only if—

(A) The study is conducted in a manner that does not permit personal identification of parents and students by individuals other than representatives of the organization that have legitimate interests in the information;

(B) The information is destroyed when no longer needed for the purposes for which the study was conducted.

(C) The educational agency or institution or the State or local educational authority or agency headed by an official listed in paragraph (a)(3) of this section enters into a written agreement with the organization that—

(1) Specifies the purpose, scope, and duration of the study or studies and the information to be disclosed;

(2) Requires the organization to use personally identifiable information from education records only to meet the purpose or purposes of the study as stated in the written agreement;

(3) Requires the organization to conduct the study in a manner that does not permit personal identification of parents and students, as defined in this part, by anyone other than representatives of the organization with legitimate interests; and

(4) Requires the organization to destroy all personally identifiable information when the information is no longer needed for the purposes for which the study was conducted and specifies the time period in which the information must be destroyed.

(iv) An educational agency or institution or State or local educational authority or Federal agency headed by an official listed in paragraph (a)(3) of this section is not required to initiate a study or agree with or endorse the conclusions or results of the study.

(v) For the purposes of paragraph (a)(6) of this section, the term "organization" includes, but is not limited to, federal, state, and local agencies, and independent organizations.

(7) The disclosure is to accrediting organizations to carry out their accrediting functions.

(8) The disclosure is to parents, as defined in § 99.3, of a dependent student, as defined in section 152 of the Internal Revenue Code of 1986.

(9)(i) The disclosure is to comply with a judicial order or lawfully issued subpoena.

(ii) The educational agency or institution may disclose information under paragraph (a)(9)(i) of this section only if the agency or institution makes a reasonable effort to notify the parent or eligible student of the order or subpoena in advance of compliance, so that the parent or eligible student may seek protective action, unless the disclosure is in compliance with—

(A) A federal grand jury subpoena and the court has ordered that the existence or the contents of the subpoena or the information furnished in response to the subpoena not be disclosed;

(B) Any other subpoena issued for a law enforcement purpose and the court or other issuing agency has ordered that the existence or the contents of the subpoena or the information furnished in response to the subpoena not be disclosed; or

(C) An *ex parte* court order obtained by the United States Attorney General (or designee not lower than an Assistant Attorney General) concerning investigations or prosecutions of an offense listed in 18 U.S.C. 2332b(g)(5)(B) or an act of domestic or international terrorism as defined in 18 U.S.C. 2331.

(iii)(A) If an educational agency or institution initiates legal action against a parent or student, the educational agency or institution may disclose to the court, without a court order or subpoena, the education records of the student that are relevant for the educational agency or institution to proceed with the legal action as plaintiff.

(B) If a parent or eligible student initiates legal action against an educational agency or institution, the educational agency or institution may disclose to the court, without a court order or subpoena, the student's education records that are relevant for the educational agency or institution to defend itself.

(10) The disclosure is in connection with a health or safety emergency, under the conditions described in § 99.36.

(11) The disclosure is information the educational agency or institution has designated as "directory information," under the conditions described in § 99.37.

(12) The disclosure is to the parent of a student who is not an eligible student or to the student.

(13) The disclosure, subject to the requirements in § 99.39, is to a victim of an alleged perpetrator of a crime of violence or a non-forcible sex offense. The disclosure may only include the final results of the disciplinary proceeding conducted by the institution of postsecondary education with respect to that alleged crime or offense. The institution may disclose the final results of the disciplinary proceeding, regardless of whether the institution concluded a violation was committed.

(14)(i) The disclosure, subject to the requirements in § 99.39, is in connection with a disciplinary proceeding at an institution of postsecondary education. The institution must not disclose the final results of the disciplinary proceeding unless it determines that—

(A) The student is an alleged perpetrator of a crime of violence or non-forcible sex offense; and

(B) With respect to the allegation made against him or her, the student has committed a violation of the institution's rules or policies.

(ii) The institution may not disclose the name of any other student, including a victim or witness, without the prior written consent of the other student.

(iii) This section applies only to disciplinary proceedings in which the final results were reached on or after October 7, 1998.

(15)(i) The disclosure is to a parent of a student at an institution of postsecondary education regarding the student's violation of any federal, state, or local law, or of any rule or policy of the institution, governing the use or possession of alcohol or a controlled substance if—

(A) The institution determines that the student has committed a disciplinary violation with respect to that use or possession; and

(B) The student is under the age of 21 at the time of the disclosure to the parent.

(ii) Paragraph (a)(15) of this section does not supersede any provision of state law that prohibits an institution of postsecondary education from disclosing information.

(16) The disclosure concerns sex offenders and other individuals required to register under section 170101 of the Violent Crime Control and Law Enforcement Act of 1994, 42 U.S.C. 14071, and the information was provided to the educational agency or institution under 42 U.S.C. 14071 and applicable federal guidelines.

(b)(1) De-identified records and information. An educational agency or institution, or a party that has received education records or information from education records under this part, may release the records or information without the consent required by §99.30 after the removal of all personally identifiable information provided that the educational agency or institution or other party has made a reasonable determination that a student's identity is not personally identifiable, whether through single or multiple releases, and taking into account other reasonably available information.

(2) An educational agency or institution, or a party that has received education records or information from education records under this part, may release de-identified student level data from education records for the purpose of education research by attaching a code to each record that may allow the recipient to match information received from the same source, provided that—

(i) An educational agency or institution or other party that releases de-identified data under paragraph (b)(2) of this section does not disclose any information about how it generates and assigns a record code, or that would allow a recipient to identify a student based on a record code;

(ii) The record code is used for no purpose other than identifying a de-identified record for purposes of education research and cannot be used to ascertain personally identifiable information about a student; and

(iii) The record code is not based on a student's social security number or other personal information.

(c) An educational agency or institution must use reasonable methods to identify and authenticate the identity of parents, students, school officials, and any other parties to whom the agency or institution discloses personally identifiable information from education records.

(d) Paragraphs (a) and (b) of this section do not require an educational agency or institution or any other party to disclose education records or information from education records to any party except for parties under paragraph (a)(12) of this section.

[Authority: 20 U.S.C. 1232g(a)(5)(A), (b), (h), (i), and (j)]

§ 99.32 WHAT RECORDKEEPING REQUIREMENTS EXIST CONCERNING REQUESTS AND DISCLOSURES?

(a)(1) An educational agency or institution must maintain a record of each request for access to and each disclosure of personally identifiable information from the education records of each student, as well as the names of State and local educational authorities and Federal officials and agencies listed in §99.31(a)(3) that may make further disclosures of personally identifiable information from the student's education records without consent under §99.33(b).

(2) The agency or institution shall maintain the record with the education records of the student as long as the records are maintained.

(3) For each request or disclosure the record must include:

(i) The parties who have requested or received personally identifiable information from the education records; and

(ii) The legitimate interests the parties had in re-questing or obtaining the information.

(4) An educational agency or institution must obtain a copy of the record of further disclosures maintained under paragraph (b)(2) of this section and make it available in response to a parent's or eligible student's request to review the record required under paragraph (a)(1) of this section.

(5) An educational agency or institution must record the following information when it discloses personally identifiable information from education records under the health or safety emergency exception in §99.31(a)(10) and §99.36:

(i) The articulable and significant threat to the health or safety of a student or other individuals that formed the basis for the disclosure; and

(ii) The parties to whom the agency or institution disclosed the information.

(b)(1) Except as provided in paragraph (b)(2) of this section, if an educational agency or institution discloses personally identifiable information from education records with the understanding authorized under §99.33(b), the record of the disclosure required under this section must include:

(i) The names of the additional parties to which the receiving party may disclose the information on behalf of the educational agency or institution; and

(ii) The legitimate interests under §99.31 which each of the additional parties has in requesting or obtaining the information.

(2)(i) A State or local educational authority or Federal official or agency listed in §99.31(a)(3) that makes further disclosures of information from education records under §99.33(b) must record the names of the additional parties to which it discloses information on behalf of an educational agency or institution and their legitimate interests in the information under §99.31 if the information was received from:

(A) An educational agency or institution that has not recorded the further disclosures under paragraph (b)(1) of this section; or

(B) Another State or local educational authority or Federal official or agency listed in §99.31(a)(3).

(ii) A State or local educational authority or Federal official or agency that records further disclosures of information under paragraph (b)(2)(i) of this section may maintain the record by the student's class, school, district, or other appropriate grouping rather than by the name of the student.

(iii) Upon request of an educational agency or institution, a State or local educational authority or Federal official or agency listed in §99.31(a)(3) that maintains a record of further disclosures under paragraph (b)(2)(i) of this section must provide a copy of the record of further disclosures to the educational agency or institution within a reasonable period of time not to exceed 30 days.

(c) The following parties may inspect the record relating to each student:

(1) The parent or eligible student.
(2) The school official or his or her assistants who are responsible for the custody of the records.
(3) Those parties authorized in § 99.3 1 (a)(1) and (3) for the purposes of auditing the recordkeeping procedures of the educational agency or institution.

(d) Paragraph (a) of this section does not apply if the request was from, or the disclosure was to:

(1) The parent or eligible student;
(2) A school official under § 99.3 1 (a)(1);
(3) A party with written consent from the parent or eligible student;
(4) A party seeking directory information; or
(5) A party seeking or receiving the records in accordance with §99.31(a)(9)(ii)(A) through (C).

(Approved by the Office of Management and Budget under control number 1880–0508)

[Authority: 20 U.S.C. 1232g(b)(1) and (b)(4)(A)]

§ 99.33 WHAT LIMITATIONS APPLY TO THE REDISCLOSURE OF INFORMATION?

(a)(1) An educational agency or institution may disclose personally identifiable information from an education record only on the condition that the party to whom the information is disclosed will not disclose the information to any other party without the prior consent of the parent or eligible student.

(2) The officers, employees, and agents of a party that receives information under paragraph (a)(1) of this section may use the information, but only for the purposes for which the disclosure was made.

(b)(1) Paragraph (a) of this section does not prevent an educational agency or institution from disclosing personally identifiable information with the understanding that the party receiving the information may make further disclosures of the information on behalf of the educational agency or institution if:

(i) The disclosures meet the requirements of § 99.31; and

(ii)(A) The educational agency or institution has complied with the requirements of § 99.32(b); or

(B) A State or local educational authority or Federal official or agency listed in §99.31(a)(3) has complied with the requirements of §99.32(b)(2).

(2) A party that receives a court order or lawfully issued subpoena and rediscloses personally identifiable information from education records on behalf of an educational agency or institution in response to that order or subpoena under §99.31(a)(9) must provide the notification required under §99.31(a)(9)(ii).

(c) Paragraph (a) of this section does not apply to disclosures under §§99.31(a)(8), (9), (11), (12), (14), (15), and (16), and to information that postsecondary institutions are required to disclose under the Jeanne Clery Disclosure of Campus Security Policy and Campus Crime Statistics Act, 20 U.S.C. 1092(f) (Clery Act), to the accuser and accused regarding the outcome of any campus disciplinary proceeding brought alleging a sexual offense.

(d) An educational agency or institution must inform a party to whom disclosure is made of the requirements of paragraph (a) of this section except for disclosures made under §§99.31(a)(8), (9), (11), (12), (14), (15), and (16), and to information that postsecondary institutions are required to disclose under the Clery Act to the accuser and accused regarding the outcome of any campus disciplinary proceeding brought alleging a sexual offense.

(e) If this Office determines that a third party outside the educational agency or institution improperly rediscloses personally identifiable information from education records in violation of this section, or fails to provide the notification required under paragraph (b)(2) of this section, the educational agency or institution may not allow that third party access to personally identifiable information from education records for at least five years.

[Authority: 20 U.S.C. 1232g(b)(4)(B)]

§ 99.34 WHAT CONDITIONS APPLY TO DISCLOSURE OF INFORMATION TO OTHER EDUCATIONAL AGENCIES OR INSTITUTIONS?

(a) An educational agency or institution that discloses an education record under § 99.31(a)(2) shall:

(1) Make a reasonable attempt to notify the parent or eligible student at the last known address of the parent or eligible student, unless:

(i) The disclosure is initiated by the parent or eligible student; or

(ii) The annual notification of the agency or institution under § 99.7 includes a notice that the agency or institution forwards education records to other agencies or institutions that have requested the records and in which the student seeks or intends to enroll or is already enrolled so long as the disclosure is for purposes related to the student's enrollment or transfer:

(2) Give the parent or eligible student, upon request, a copy of the record that was disclosed; and

(3) Give the parent or eligible student, upon request, an opportunity for a hearing under Subpart C.

(b) An educational agency or institution may disclose an education record of a student in attendance to another educational agency or institution if:

(1) The student is enrolled in or receives services from the other agency or institution; and

(2) The disclosure meets the requirements of paragraph (a) of this section.

[Authority: 20 U.S.C. 1232g(b)(1)(B)]

§ 99.35 WHAT CONDITIONS APPLY TO DISCLOSURE OF INFORMATION FOR FEDERAL OR STATE PROGRAM PURPOSES?

(a)(1) Authorized representatives of the officials or agencies headed by officials listed in §99.31(a)(3) may have access to education records in connection with an audit or evaluation of federal or state supported education programs, or for the enforcement of or compliance with federal legal requirements that relate to those programs.

(2) The State or local educational authority or agency headed by an official listed in §99.31(a)(3) is responsible for using reasonable methods to ensure to the greatest extent practicable that any entity or individual designated as its authorized representative—

(i) Uses personally identifiable information only to carry out an audit or evaluation of Federal- or State-supported education programs, or for the enforcement of or compliance with Federal legal requirements related to these programs;

(ii) Protects the personally identifiable information from further disclosures or other uses, except as authorized in paragraph (b)(1) of this section; and

(iii) Destroys the personally identifiable information in accordance with the requirements of paragraphs (b) and (c) of this section.

(3) The State or local educational authority or agency headed by an official listed in §99.31(a)(3) must use a written agreement to designate any authorized representative, other than an employee. The written agreement must—

(i) Designate the individual or entity as an authorized representative;

(ii) Specify—

(A) The personally identifiable information from education records to be disclosed;

(B) That the purpose for which the personally identifiable information from education records is disclosed to the authorized representative is to carry out an audit or evaluation of Federal- or State-supported education programs, or to enforce or to comply with Federal legal requirements that relate to those programs; and

(C) A description of the activity with sufficient specificity to make clear that the work falls within the exception of §99.31(a)(3), including a description of how the personally identifiable information from education records will be used;

(iii) Require the authorized representative to destroy personally identifiable information from education records when the information is no longer needed for the purpose specified;

(iv) Specify the time period in which the information must be destroyed; and

(v) Establish policies and procedures, consistent with the Act and other Federal and State confidentiality and privacy provisions, to protect personally identifiable information from education records from further disclosure (except back to the disclosing entity) and unauthorized use, including limiting use of personally identifiable information from education records to only authorized representatives with legitimate interests in the audit or evaluation of a Federal- or State-supported education program or for compliance or enforcement of Federal legal requirements related to these programs.

(b) Information that is collected under paragraph (a) of this section must—

(1) Be protected in a manner that does not permit personal identification of individuals by anyone other than the State or local educational authority or agency headed by an official listed in §99.31(a)(3) and their authorized representatives, except that the State or local educational authority or agency headed by an official listed in §99.31(a)(3) may make further disclosures of personally identifiable information from education records on behalf of the educational agency or institution in accordance with the requirements of §99.33(b); and

(2) Be destroyed when no longer needed for the purposes listed in paragraph (a) of this section.

(c) Paragraph (b) of this section does not apply if:

(1) The parent or eligible student has given written consent for the disclosure under § 99.30; or
(2) The collection of personally identifiable information is specifically authorized by federal law.

[Authority: 20 U.S.C. 1232g(b)(3)]

§ 99.36 WHAT CONDITIONS APPLY TO DISCLOSURE OF INFORMATION IN HEALTH AND SAFETY EMERGENCIES?

(a) An educational agency or institution may disclose personally identifiable information from an education record to appropriate parties, including parents of an eligible student, in connection with an emergency if knowledge of the information is necessary to protect the health or safety of the student or other individuals.
(b) Nothing in the *Act* or this part shall prevent an educational agency or institution from-

(1) Including in the education records of a student appropriate information concerning disciplinary action taken against the student for conduct that posed a significant risk to the safety or well-being of that student, other students, or other members of the school community;
(2) Disclosing appropriate information maintained under paragraph (b)(1) of this section to teachers and school officials within the agency or institution who the agency or institution has determined have legitimate educational interests in the behavior of the student; or
(3) Disclosing appropriate information maintained under paragraph (b)(1) of this section to teachers and school officials in other schools who have been determined to have legitimate educational interests in the behavior of the student.

(c) In making a determination under paragraph (a) of this section, an educational agency or institution may take into account the totality of the circumstances pertaining to a threat to the health or safety of a student or other individuals. If the educational agency or institution determines that there is an articulable and significant threat to the health or safety of a student or other individuals, it may disclose information from education records to any person whose knowledge of the information is necessary to protect the health or safety of the student or other individuals. If, based on the information available at the time of the determination, there is a rational basis for the determination, the Department will not substitute its judgment for that of the educational agency or institution in evaluating the circumstances and making its determination.

[Authority: 20 U.S.C. 1232g(b)(1)(I) and (h)]

§ 99.37 WHAT CONDITIONS APPLY TO DISCLOSING DIRECTORY INFORMATION?

(a) An educational agency or institution may disclose directory information if it has given public notice to parents of students in attendance and eligible students in attendance at the agency or institution of:

(1) The types of personally identifiable information that the agency or institution has designated as directory information;
(2) A parent's or eligible student's right to refuse to let the agency or institution designate any or all of those types of information about the student as directory information; and
(3) The period of time within which a parent or eligible student has to notify the agency or institution in writing that he or she does not want any or all of those types of information about the student designated as directory information.

(b) An educational agency or institution may disclose directory information about former students without meeting the conditions in paragraph (a) of this section. However, the agency or institution must continue to honor any valid request to opt out of the disclosure of directory information made while a student was in attendance unless the student rescinds the opt out request.

(c) A parent or eligible student may not use the right under paragraph (a)(2) of this section to opt out of directory information disclosures to—

(1) prevent an educational agency or institution from disclosing or requiring a student to disclose the student's name, identifier, or institutional email address in a class in which the student is enrolled; or

(2) Prevent an educational agency or institution from requiring a student to wear, to display publicly, or to disclose a student ID card or badge that exhibits information that may be designated as directory information under §99.3 and that has been properly designated by the educational agency or institution as directory information in the public notice provided under paragraph (a)(1) of this section.

(d) In its public notice to parents and eligible students in attendance at the agency or institution that is described in paragraph (a) of this section, an educational agency or institution may specify that disclosure of directory information will be limited to specific parties, for specific purposes, or both. When an educational agency or institution specifies that disclosure of directory information will be limited to specific parties, for specific purposes, or both, the educational agency or institution must limit its directory information disclosures to those specified in its public notice that is described in paragraph (a) of this section.

(e) An educational agency or institution may not disclose or confirm directory information without meeting the written consent requirements in §99.30 if a student's social security number or other non-directory information is used alone or combined with other data elements to identify or help identify the student or the student's records.

[Authority: 20 U.S.C. 1232g(a)(5)(A) and (B)]

§ 99.38 WHAT CONDITIONS APPLY TO DISCLOSURE OF INFORMATION AS PERMITTED BY STATE STATUTE ADOPTED AFTER NOVEMBER 19, 1974 CONCERNING THE JUVENILE JUSTICE SYSTEM?

(a) If reporting or disclosure allowed by state statute concerns the juvenile justice system and the system's ability to effectively serve, prior to adjudication, the student whose records are released, an educational agency or institution may disclose education records under § 99.31(a)(5)(i)(B).

(b) The officials and authorities to whom the records are disclosed shall certify in writing to the educational agency or institution that the information will not be disclosed to any other party, except as provided under state law, without the prior written consent of the parent of the student.

[Authority: 20 U.S.C. 1232g(b)(1)(J)]

§ 99.39 WHAT DEFINITIONS APPLY TO THE NONCONSENSUAL DISCLOSURE OF RECORDS BY POSTSECONDARY EDUCATIONAL INSTITUTIONS IN CONNECTION WITH DISCIPLINARY PROCEEDINGS CONCERNING CRIMES OF VIOLENCE OR NON-FORCIBLE SEX OFFENSES?

As used in this part:

ALLEGED PERPETRATOR OF A CRIME OF VIOLENCE is a student who is alleged to have committed acts that would, if proven, constitute any of the following offenses or attempts to commit the following offenses that are defined in appendix A to this part:

- Arson
- Assault offenses
- Burglary
- Criminal homicide—manslaughter by negligence
- Criminal homicide—murder and nonnegligent manslaughter
- Destruction/damage/vandalism of property
- Kidnapping/abduction
- Robbery
- Forcible sex offenses

ALLEGED PERPETRATOR OF A NONFORCIBLE SEX OFFENSE means a student who is alleged to have committed acts that, if proven, would constitute statutory rape or incest. These offenses are defined in Appendix A to this part.

FINAL RESULTS means a decision or determination, made by an honor court or council, committee, commission, or other entity authorized to resolve disciplinary matters within the institution. The disclosure of final results must include only the name of the student, the violation committed, and any sanction imposed by the institution against the student.

SANCTION IMPOSED means a description of the disciplinary action taken by the institution, the date of its imposition, and its duration.

VIOLATION COMMITTED means the institutional rules or code sections that were violated and any essential findings supporting the institution's conclusion that the violation was committed.

[Authority: 20 U.S.C. 1232g(b)(6)]

Subpart E—What Are the Enforcement Procedures?

§ 99.60 WHAT FUNCTIONS HAS THE SECRETARY DELEGATED TO THE OFFICE AND TO THE OFFICE OF ADMINISTRATIVE LAW JUDGES?

(a) For the purposes of this subpart, "Office" means the Family Policy Compliance Office, U.S. Department of Education.

(b) The Secretary designates the Office to:

(1) Investigate, process, and review complaints and violations under the *Act* and this part; and

(2) Provide technical assistance to ensure compliance with the *Act* and this part.

(c) The Secretary designates the Office of Administrative Law Judges to act as the Review Board required under the *Act* to enforce the *Act* with respect to all applicable programs. The term "applicable program" is defined in section 400 of the *General Education Provisions Act*.

[Authority: 20 U.S.C. 1232g(f) and (g), 1234]

§ 99.61 WHAT RESPONSIBILITY DOES AN EDUCATIONAL AGENCY OR INSTITUTION HAVE CONCERNING CONFLICT WITH STATE OR LOCAL LAWS?

If an educational agency or institution determines that it cannot comply with the *Act* or this part due to a conflict with state or local law, it must notify the Office within 45 days, giving the text and citation of the conflicting law. If another recipient of Department funds under any program administered by the Secretary or a third party to which personally identifiable information from education records has been non-consensually disclosed determines that it cannot comply with the Act or this part due to a conflict with State or local law, it also must notify the Office within 45 days, giving the text and citation of the conflicting law.

[Authority: 20 U.S.C. 1232g(f)]

§ 99.62 WHAT INFORMATION MUST AN EDUCATIONAL AGENCY OR INSTITUTION SUBMIT TO THE OFFICE?

The Office may require an educational agency or institution, other recipient of Department funds under any program administered by the Secretary to which personally identifiable information from education records is non-consensually disclosed, or any third party outside of an educational agency or institution to which personally identifiable information from education records is non-consensually disclosed to submit reports, information on policies and procedures, annual notifications, training materials, and other information necessary to carry out its enforcement responsibilities under the Act or this part.

[Authority: 20 U.S.C. 1232g(f) and (g)]

§ 99.63 WHERE ARE COMPLAINTS FILED?

A parent or eligible student may file a written complaint with the Office regarding an alleged violation under the *Act* and this part. The Office's address is: Family Policy Compliance Office, U.S. Department of Education, 400 Maryland Avenue, SW, Washington, D.C. 20202–4605.

[Authority: 20 U.S.C. 1232g(g)]

§ 99.64 WHAT IS THE INVESTIGATION PROCEDURE?

(a) A complaint must contain specific allegations of fact giving reasonable cause to believe that a violation of the *Act* or this part has occurred. A complaint does not have to allege that a violation is based on a policy or practice of the educational agency or institution, other recipient of Department funds under any program administered by the Secretary, or any third party outside of an educational agency or institution.

(b) The Office investigates a timely complaint filed by a parent or eligible student, or conducts its own investigation when no complaint has been filed or a complaint has been withdrawn, to determine whether an educational agency or institution or other recipient of Department funds under any program administered by the Secretary has failed to comply with a provision of the Act or this part. If the Office determines that an educational agency or institution or other recipient of Department funds under any program administered by the Secretary has failed to comply with a provision of the Act or this part, it may also determine whether the failure to comply is based on a policy or practice of the agency or institution or other recipient. The Office also investigates a timely complaint filed by a parent or eligible student, or conducts its own investigation when no complaint has been filed or a complaint has been withdrawn, to determine whether a third party outside of the educational agency or institution has failed to comply with the provisions of §99.31(a)(6)(iii)(B) or has improperly redisclosed personally identifiable information from education records in violation of §99.33.

(c) A timely complaint is defined as an allegation of a violation of the *Act* that is submitted to the Office within 180 days of the date of the alleged violation or of the date that the complainant knew or reasonably should have known of the alleged violation.

(d) The Office may extend the time limit in this section for good cause shown.

[Authority: 20 U.S.C. 1232g(f)]

§ 99.65 WHAT IS THE CONTENT OF THE NOTICE OF INVESTIGATION ISSUED BY THE OFFICE?

(a) The Office notifies in writing the complainant, if any, and the educational agency or institution, the recipient of Department funds under any program administered by the Secretary, or the third party outside of an educational agency or institution if it initiates an investigation under §99.64(b). The written notice—

(1) Includes the substance of the allegations against the educational agency or institution, other recipient, or third party; and

(2) Directs the agency or institution, other recipient, or third party to submit a written response and other relevant information, as set forth in §99.62, within a specified period of time, including information about its policies and practices regarding education records.

(b) The Office notifies the complainant if it does not initiate an investigation of a complaint because the complaint fails to meet the requirements of § 99.64.

[Authority: 20 U.S.C. 1232g(g)]

§ 99.66 WHAT ARE THE RESPONSIBILITIES OF THE OFFICE IN THE ENFORCEMENT PROCESS?

(a) The Office reviews the complaint, if any, information submitted by the educational agency or institution, other recipient of Department funds under any program administered by the Secretary, or third party outside of an educational agency or institution, and any other relevant information. The Office may permit the parties to submit further written or oral arguments or information.

(b) Following its investigation, the Office provides to the complainant, if any, and the educational agency or institution, other recipient, or third party a written notice of its findings and the basis for its findings.

(c) If the Office finds that an educational agency or institution or other recipient has not complied with a provision of the *Act* or this part, it may also find that the failure to comply was based on a policy or practice of the agency or institution or other recipient. A notice of findings issued under paragraph (b) of this section to an educational agency or institution, or other recipient that has not complied with a provision of the Act or this part—

(1) Includes a statement of the specific steps that the agency or institution or other recipient must take to comply; and

(2) Provides a reasonable period of time, given all of the circumstances of the case, during which the educational agency or institution or other recipient may comply voluntarily.

(d) If the Office finds that a third party outside of an educational agency or institution has not complied with the provisions of §99.31(a)(6)(iii)(B) or has improperly redisclosed personally identifiable information from education records in violation of §99.33, the Office's notice of findings issued under paragraph (b) of this section—

(1) Includes a statement of the specific steps that the third party outside of the educational agency or institution must take to comply; and

(2) Provides a reasonable period of time, given all of the circumstances of the case, during which the third party may comply voluntarily.

[Authority: 20 U.S.C. 1232g(b)(4)(B), (f), and (g)]

§ 99.67 HOW DOES THE SECRETARY ENFORCE DECISIONS?

(a) If an educational agency or institution or other recipient of Department funds under any program administered by the Secretary does not comply during the period of time set under § 99.66(c), the Secretary may take any legally available enforcement action in accordance with the Act, including, but not limited to, the following enforcement actions available in accordance with part D of the *General Education Provisions Act*—

(1) Withhold further payments under any applicable program;
(2) Issue a complaint to compel compliance through a cease-and-desist order; or
(3) Terminate eligibility to receive funding under any applicable program.

(b) If, after an investigation under § 99.66, the Secretary finds that an educational agency or institution, other recipient, or third party has complied voluntarily with the *Act* or this part, the Secretary provides the complainant and the agency or institution, other recipient, or third party with written notice of the decision and the basis for the decision.

(c) If the Office finds that a third party, outside the educational agency or institution, violates §99.31(a)(6)(iii)(B), then the educational agency or institution from which the personally identifiable information originated may not allow the third party found to be responsible for the violation of §99.31(a)(6)(iii)(B) access to personally identifiable information from education records for at least five years.

(d) If the Office finds that a State or local educational authority, a Federal agency headed by an official listed in §99.31(a)(3), or an authorized representative of a State or local educational authority or a Federal agency headed by an official listed in §99.31(a)(3), improperly rediscloses personally identifiable information from education records, then the educational agency or institution from which the personally identifiable information originated may not allow the third party found to be responsible for the improper redisclosure access to personally identifiable information from education records for at least five years.

(e) If the Office finds that a third party, outside the educational agency or institution, improperly rediscloses personally identifiable information from education records in violation of §99.33 or fails to provide the notification required under §99.33(b)(2), then the educational agency or institution from which the personally identifiable information originated may not allow the third party found to be responsible for the violation access to personally identifiable information from education records for at least five years.

[Authority: 20 U.S.C. 1232g (b)(4)(B) and (f); 20 U.S.C. 1234c]

Appendix A to Part 99—Crimes of Violence Definitions

ARSON: Any willful or malicious burning or attempt to burn, with or without intent to defraud, a dwelling house, public building, motor vehicle or aircraft, personal property of another, etc.

ASSAULT OFFENSES: An unlawful attack by one person upon another.

Note: By definition there can be no "attempted" assaults, only "completed" assaults.

(a) *Aggravated Assault.* An unlawful attack by one person upon another for the purpose of inflicting severe or aggravated bodily injury. This type of assault usually is accompanied by the use of a weapon or by means likely to produce death or great bodily harm. (It is not necessary that injury result from an aggravated assault when a gun, knife, or other weapon is used which could and probably would result in serious injury if the crime were successfully completed.)

(b) *Simple Assault.* An unlawful physical attack by one person upon another where neither the offender displays a weapon, nor the victim suffers obvious severe or aggravated bodily injury involving apparent broken bones, loss of teeth, possible internal injury, severe laceration, or loss of consciousness.

(c) *Intimidation.* To unlawfully place another person in reasonable fear of bodily harm through the use of threatening words or other conduct, or both, but without displaying a weapon or subjecting the victim to actual physical attack.

Note: This offense includes stalking.

BURGLARY: The unlawful entry into a building or other structure with the intent to commit a felony or a theft.

CRIMINAL HOMICIDE—MANSLAUGHTER BY NEGLIGENCE: The killing of another person through gross negligence.

CRIMINAL HOMICIDE—MURDER AND NONNEGLIGENT MANSLAUGHTER: The willful (non-negligent) killing of one human being by another.

DESTRUCTION/DAMAGE/VANDALISM OF PROPERTY: To willfully or maliciously destroy, damage, deface, or otherwise injure real or personal property without the consent of the owner or the person having custody or control of it.

KIDNAPPING/ABDUCTION: The unlawful seizure, transportation, or detention of a person, or any combination of these actions, against his or her will, or of a minor without the consent of his or her custodial parent(s) or legal guardian.

Note: Kidnapping/Abduction includes hostage taking.

ROBBERY: The taking of, or attempting to take, anything of value under confrontational circumstances from the control, custody, or care of a person or persons by force or threat of force or violence or by putting the victim in fear.

Note: Carjackings are robbery offenses where a motor vehicle is taken through force or threat of force.

SEX OFFENSES, FORCIBLE: Any sexual act directed against another person, forcibly or against that person's will, or both; or not forcibly or against the person's will where the victim is incapable of giving consent.

(a) *Forcible Rape* (Except "Statutory Rape"). The carnal knowledge of a person, forcibly or against that person's will, or both; or not forcibly or against the person's will where the victim is incapable of giving consent because of his or her temporary or permanent mental or physical incapacity (or because of his or her youth).

(b) *Forcible Sodomy.* Oral or anal sexual intercourse with another person, forcibly or against that person's will, or both; or not forcibly or against the person's will where the victim is incapable of giving consent because of his or her youth or because of his or her temporary or permanent mental or physical incapacity.

(c) *Sexual Assault with an Object.* To use an object or instrument to unlawfully penetrate, however slightly, the genital or anal opening of the body of another person, forcibly or against that person's will, or both; or not forcibly or against the person's will where the victim is incapable of giving consent because of his or her youth or because of his or her temporary or permanent mental or physical incapacity.

Note: An "object" or "instrument" is anything used by the offender other than the offender's genitalia. Examples are a finger, bottle, handgun, stick, etc.

(d) *Forcible Fondling.* The touching of the private body parts of another person for the purpose of sexual gratification, forcibly or against that person's will, or both; or not forcibly or against the person's will where the victim is incapable of giving consent because of his or her youth or because of his or her temporary or permanent mental or physical incapacity.

Note: Forcible Fondling includes "Indecent Liberties" and "Child Molesting."

NONFORCIBLE SEX OFFENSES (EXCEPT "PROSTITUTION OFFENSES"): Unlawful, nonforcible sexual intercourse.

(a) *Incest.* Nonforcible sexual intercourse between persons who are related to each other within the degrees wherein marriage is prohibited by law.

(b) *Statutory Rape.* Nonforcible sexual intercourse with a person who is under the statutory age of consent.

[Authority: 20 U.S.C. 1232g(b)(6) and 18 U.S.C. 16]

[This is not an official version of the regulations. These regulations are codified in 34 C.F.R. Part 99.]

[Updated January 2012.]

APPENDIX B

FERPA Section-by-Section Analysis

2012 Amendments

The Department of Education's official summary during the presentation of the final regulations in December 2011 explains that these amendments were requisite for the effective use of data in connection with States' ability to "evaluate education programs, to ensure limited resources are invested effectively, to build upon what works and discard what does not, to increase accountability and transparency, and to contribute to a culture of innovation and continuous improvement in education." The Department also explained that it attempted to achieve a balance between using the benefits of student data with the need to protect students' privacy. The following is a section-by-section analysis of the changes made *effective on January 3, 2012*.

$99.3 DEFINITIONS

AUTHORIZED REPRESENTATIVE is defined as any entity or individual designated by a State or local educational authority or the Comptroller General, the Attorney General, or the Secretary of the Department of Education to conduct evaluation or audit studies, or any compliance and enforcement activity in connection Federal legal requirements. These individuals or entities have broader power for requests of disclosure from education records relative to school officials. By defining the term, the department has made the new emphasis on data sharing and educational evaluation more clear.

EDUCATION PROGRAM is defined in broad terms to ensure that no program that is "principally" engaged in the provision of education is excluded. This new definition facilitates States' compliance with America Creating Opportunities to Meaningfully Promote Excellence in Technology, Education, and Science (COMPETES) Act and other legislation designed to improve educational provisions in America, by facilitating the disclosure of personally identifiable information from education records, as necessary, to evaluate and audit a broad category of education programs.

DIRECTORY INFORMATION has been amended to clarify that student identification numbers may be classified as directory information for the purposes of display on a student ID card or badge so long as the number cannot be used alone to access information from education records without the use of one or more factors that authenticate the user's identity which are only known to the authorized user. Notably, an eligible student may *not* opt out of wearing ID badges, though they may opt-out from other directory information disclosures.

§99.31(A)(6) ORGANIZATIONS CONDUCTING STUDIES

This section has been amended to clarify that FERPA-permitted entities are *not* prevented from redisclosing personally identifiable information from education records to researchers who conduct evaluative or audit studies for or on behalf of the institution. This change was made to make data sharing easier in the cause of using that data to improve existing education programs. However, in the interests of maintaining student privacy, the records must be destroyed once the information is no longer needed in connection with the study being conducted. The time period in which the records are destroyed must be recorded also.

DISCLOSURE OF INFORMATION FOR FEDERAL AND STATE PROGRAMS

§99.35(A)(2) has been amended to remove the requirement that any FERPA-permitted entities must have legal authority to conduct audit, evaluation, or enforcement or compliance activity. This change was made to clarify that Federal, State, and local law determine whether a given audit or evaluation is permitted, not FERPA. Therefore, authority for a FERPA-permitted entity to conduct studies for either audit or evaluative purposes, or in connection with enforcement or compliance activity, may be *express or implied.*

§99.35(A)(3) now requires that FERPA-permitted entities use written agreements to designate authorized representatives, other than employees, that allow the authorized representative access to personally identifiable information from education records without prior written consent in connection with evaluative studies or compliance or enforcement activity. This written agreement, along with "reasonable methods," is designed to ensure to the greatest extent practicable FERPA compliance. This also limits the usage of PII by the authorized representative, to protect student privacy without creating extensive bureaucratic obstacles to conducting studies.

§99.35(D) is a new section which stipulates that if the Family Policy Compliance Office[1] finds an improper redisclosure has been made, it will prohibit the original educational agency or institution which disclosed the PII from disclosing to the offending entities for a period of not less than five years. This amendment is intended to discourage the improper use of student data, promoting its use only as a tool in the improvement of educational agencies and institutions. It is a necessary enforcement activity considering the increased amount of student data that will be available to a variety of FERPA-permitted entities.

§99.37(C) STUDENT IDENTIFICATION AND COMMUNICATION IN CLASS

This section has been amended to clarify further, that parents or eligible students may opt out of disclosure of directory information, but this will not prevent an institution from requiring students to wear or carry ID badges that exhibits directory information as set forth in §99.3 "Directory Information."

§99.37(D) USE OF SSNS

This section has been amended to clarify that educational agencies or institutions may develop policies that allow the disclosure of directory information only to specific parties, for specific purposes, or both. All exceptions to written consent to disclosure set forth in §99.31 are optional—the only people

[1] As of 2017, the office that currently administers FERPA-related issues is the Student Privacy Policy Office.

required access to their education records are eligible students and parents of non-eligible students.

This change assists educational agencies and institutions in protecting directory information since the option is left open to disclose to only a set group of entities, for a set group of reasons, or both, as set forth in its Directory Information Notice.

§ 99.62, § 99.64, § 99.65, § 99.66, § 99.67 ENFORCEMENT PROVISIONS

These have been changed extensively to make the Department of Education, in general, and the Family Policy Compliance Office[2] specifically, more powerful in enforcing and penalizing entities for inappropriate disclosure and misuse of data. The Secretary of Education can take appropriate actions to enforce FERPA against *any entity that receives funds under any program administered by the Secretary, including funds provided by grant, cooperative agreement, contract, subgrant, or subcontract.* This description affects all fitting entities regardless of whether they have students in attendance or not. This addition reflects the broader power the Department of Education now possess to counteract any misuse of the more widely available and obtainable student data.

§99.66 (D) is added to deal with enforcement of infractions by third parties, since previously only educational institutions and agencies were subject to enforcement by FERPA. It provides the entity with a set of instructions on how to comply and a reasonable amount of time that the entity will have to comply voluntarily.

§99.67 (C), (D), AND (E) address the penalty for noncompliance with FERPA in connection with committing improper disclosure or redisclosure by SEAs, LEA's authorized representatives of these entities or of federal agencies, or any other third parties. If the Department finds this to be the case, then the offending entity is prohibited from receiving disclosures from the original disclosing institution or agency for a period of not less than five years.

[2] As of 2017, the office that currently administers FERPA-related issues is the Student Privacy Policy Office.

APPENDIX C

Major Points Summarizing the 2012 Regulatory Changes

The following points summarize the major revisions from the 2012 amendments. (*See* Appendix A for an annotated version of the Regulations.)

- Expanding the definition of "authorized representative" to include any entity or individual designated by a State or location educational authority or an agency headed by an official listed in 99.31 (a)(3) to conduct—with respect to Federal or State supported education programs—any audit, evaluation, or compliance or enforcement activity in connection with Federal legal requirements that relates to these programs. (§99.3)
- Clarifying that an education program means any program that is principally engaged in the provision of education, including but not limited to, early childhood education, elementary and secondary education, job training, career and technical education, and adult education, and any program that is administered by an educational agency or institution. (§99.3)
- Clarifying that displaying a student ID number on a student ID badge is acceptable, but only if the identified cannot be used to gain access to education records except when used in conjunction with one or more factors that authenticate the user's identity. (§99.3)
- Clarifying that FERPA does not prevent a State or local educational authority or agency headed by an official listed in the Act from entering into agreements with organizations conducting studies that would necessitate

rediscloosing personally identifiable information from education records on behalf of educational agencies and institutions that disclosed the information to the State or Local educational authority or agency. (§99.31)

- Outlining that a State or local educational authority or agency headed by an official listed in 99.31(a)(3) is responsible for ensuring that its authorized representatives use personally identifiable information only to carry out an audit or evaluation of Federal- or State-supported education programs, to protect the information from further disclosure or other uses, and destroys the information when no longer needed for the purposes originally stated. (§99.31)
- Stating that written agreements must be used to designate any authorized representative who isn't an employee. The written agreement must specify: (a) the information to be disclosed, (b) the audit or evaluation purpose of the disclosure, and (c) require the destruction of the data when it has been used for the intended purpose. (§99.35)
- Allowing for an institution to specify that disclosure of directory information will be limited to specific parties, for specific purposes, or both. Any such limit on the use of directory information must be included in the institution's directory information notice to students. (§99.37)

Copies of the original 1974 law, as amended, as well as the final regulations, are included in Appendices A and B of this publication. The reader should always check to see if the Department of Education has issued any regulations since publication of this Guide through the web page of the Student Privacy Policy Office (SPPO), the office in the Department of Education that is currently responsible for administering FERPA, at: <ed.gov/policy/gen/guid/fpco/> or <aacrao.org/ferpa>.

APPENDIX D

Model Notification of Rights under FERPA for Postsecondary Institutions

The Family Educational Rights and Privacy Act (FERPA) affords eligible students certain rights with respect to their education records. (An "eligible student" under FERPA is a student who is 18 years of age or older or who attends a postsecondary institution.) These rights include:

- The right to inspect and review the student's education records within 45 days after the day the [Name of postsecondary institution ("School")] receives a request for access. A student should submit to the registrar, dean, head of the academic department, or other appropriate official, a written request that identifies the record(s) the student wishes to inspect. The school official will make arrangements for access and notify the student of the time and place where the records may be inspected. If the records are not maintained by the school official to whom the request was submitted, that official shall advise the student of the correct official to whom the request should be addressed.
- The right to request the amendment of the student's education records that the student believes is inaccurate, misleading, or otherwise in violation of the student's privacy rights under FERPA.

  A student who wishes to ask the school to amend a record should write the school official responsible for the record, clearly identify the part of the record the student wants changed, and specify why it should be changed.

  If the school decides not to amend the record as requested, the school will notify the student in writing of the decision and the student's right to a hearing regarding the request for amendment. Additional information regarding the hearing procedures will be provided to the student when notified of the right to a hearing.

- The right to provide written consent before the university discloses personally identifiable information (PII) from the student's education records, except to the extent that FERPA authorizes disclosure without consent.

  The school discloses education records without a student's prior written consent under the FERPA exception for disclosure to school officials with legitimate educational interests. A school official is a person employed by the [School] in an administrative, supervisory, academic, research, or support staff position (including law enforcement unit personnel and health staff); a person serving on the board of trustees; or a student serving on an official committee, such as a disciplinary or grievance committee. A school official also may include a volunteer or contractor outside of the [School] who performs an institutional service of function for which the school would otherwise use its own employees and who is under the direct control of the school with respect to the use and maintenance of PII from education records, such as an attorney, auditor, or collection agent or a student volunteering to assist another school official in performing their tasks. A school official has a legitimate educational interest if the official needs to review an education record in order to fulfill their professional responsibilities for the [School].

  [Optional] Upon request, the school also discloses education records without consent to officials of another school in which a student seeks or intends to enroll. [*Note to Postsecondary Institution:* FERPA requires a school to make a reasonable attempt to notify each student of these disclosures unless the school states in its annual notification that it intends to forward records on request.]

- The right to file a complaint with the U.S. Department of Education concerning alleged failures by the [School] to comply with the requirements of FERPA. The name and address of the Office that administers FERPA is:

Student Privacy Policy Office
U.S. Department of Education
400 Maryland Avenue, SW
Washington, DC 20202

[*Note*: In addition, a school may want to include its directory information public notice, as required by §99.37 of the regulations, with its annual notification of rights under FERPA.]

[Optional] See the list below of the disclosures that postsecondary institutions may make without consent.

FERPA permits the disclosure of personally identifiable information (PII) from students' education records, without consent of the student, if the disclosure meets certain conditions found in §99.31 of the FERPA regulations. Except for disclosures to school officials, disclosures related to some judicial orders or lawfully issued subpoenas, disclosures of directory information, and disclosures to the student, §99.32 of FERPA regulations requires the institution to record the disclosure. Eligible students have a right to inspect and review the record of disclosures. A postsecondary institution may disclose PII from the education records without obtaining prior written consent of the student—

- To other school officials, including teachers, within the [School] whom the school has determined to have legitimate educational interests. This includes contractors, consultants, volunteers, or other parties to whom the school has outsourced institutional services or functions, provided that the conditions listed in §99.31(a)(1)(i)(B)(1)–(a)(1)(i)(B)(2) are met. (§99.31(a)(1))
- To officials of another school where the student seeks or intends to enroll, or where the student is already enrolled if the disclosure is for purposes related to the student's enrollment or transfer, subject to the requirements of §99.34. (§99.31(a)(2))
- To authorized representatives of the U. S. Comptroller General, the U. S. Attorney General, the U.S. Secretary of Education, or State and local educational authorities, such as a State postsecondary authority that is responsible for supervising the university's State-supported education programs. Disclosures under this provision may be made, subject to the requirements of §99.35, in connection with an audit or evaluation of Federal- or State-supported education programs, or for the enforcement of or compliance with Federal legal requirements that relate to those programs. These entities may make further disclosures of PII to outside entities that are designated by them as their authorized representatives to conduct any

audit, evaluation, or enforcement or compliance activity on their behalf. (§§99.31(a)(3) and 99.35)

- In connection with financial aid for which the student has applied or which the student has received, if the information is necessary to determine eligibility for the aid, determine the amount of the aid, determine the conditions of the aid, or enforce the terms and conditions of the aid. (§99.31(a)(4))
- To organizations conducting studies for, or on behalf of, the school, in order to: (a) develop, validate, or administer predictive tests; (b) administer student aid programs; or (c) improve instruction. (§99.31(a)(6))
- To accrediting organizations to carry out their accrediting functions. ((§99.31(a)(7))
- To parents of an eligible student if the student is a dependent for IRS tax purposes. (§99.31(a)(8))
- To comply with a judicial order or lawfully issued subpoena. (§99.31(a)(9))
- To appropriate officials in connection with a health or safety emergency, subject to §99.36. (§99.31(a)(10))
- Information the school has designated as "directory information" under §99.37. (§99.31(a)(11))
- To a victim of an alleged perpetrator of a crime of violence or a non-forcible sex offense, subject to the requirements of §99.39. The disclosure may only include the final results of the disciplinary proceeding with respect to that alleged crime or offense, regardless of the finding. (§99.31(a)(13))
- To the general public, the final results of a disciplinary proceeding, subject to the requirements of §99.39, if the school determines the student is an alleged perpetrator of a crime of violence or non-forcible sex offense and the student has committed a violation of the school's rules or policies with respect to the allegation made against him or her. (§99.31(a)(14))
- To parents of a student regarding the student's violation of any Federal, State, or local law, or of any rule or policy of the school, governing the use or possession of alcohol or a controlled substance if the school determines the student committed a disciplinary violation and the student is under the age of 21. (§99.31(a)(15))
- The disclosure concerns sex offenders and other individuals required to register under section 17010 of the Violent Crime Control and Law Enforcement Act of 1994.

In light of the changes incorporated in the 2012 FERPA regulations which allow extensive redisclosure of student education records by parties listed in 99.31(a)(3) and 99.31(a)(6), AACRAO contracted with a prominent D.C. law firm to produce language, which institutions may wish to include as an addition to their annual FERPA Notice.

FERPA Annual Notice Addendum

As of January 3, 2012, the U.S. Department of Education's FERPA regulations expand the circumstances under which your education records and personally identifiable information (PII) contained in such records — including your Social Security Number, grades, or other private information—may be accessed without your consent. First, the U.S. Comptroller General, the U.S. Attorney General, the U.S. Secretary of Education, or state and local education authorities ("Federal and State Authorities") may allow access to your records and PII without your consent to any third party designated by a Federal or State Authority to evaluate a federal- or state-supported education program. The evaluation may relate to any program that is "principally engaged in the provision of education," such as early childhood education and job training, as well as any program that is administered by an education agency or institution. Second, Federal and State Authorities may allow access to your education records and PII without your consent to researchers performing certain types of studies, in certain cases even when we object to or do not request such research. Federal and State Authorities must obtain certain use-restriction and data security promises from the entities that they authorize to receive your PII, but the Authorities need not maintain direct control over such entities. In addition, in connection with Statewide Longitudinal Data Systems, State Authorities may collect, compile, permanently retain, and share without your consent PII from your education records, and they may track your participation in education and other programs by linking such PII to other personal information about you that they obtain from other Federal or State data sources, including workforce development, unemployment insurance, child welfare, juvenile justice, military service, and migrant student records systems.

APPENDIX E

FPCO/SPPO Guidance Brochure for Colleges

Balancing Student Privacy and School Safety: A Guide to the Family Educational Rights and Privacy Act for Colleges and Universities[1]

Postsecondary officials are regularly asked to balance the interests of safety and privacy for individual students. While the *Family Educational Rights and Privacy Act* (FERPA) generally requires institutions to ask for written consent before disclosing a student's personally identifiable information, it also allows colleges and universities to take key steps to maintain campus safety. Understanding the law empowers school officials to act decisively and quickly when issues arise.

HEALTH OR SAFETY EMERGENCY

In an emergency, FERPA permits school officials to disclose without student consent education records, including personally identifiable information from those records, to protect the health or safety of students or other individuals. At such times, records and information may be released to appropriate parties such as law enforcement officials, public health officials, and trained medical personnel. *See* 34 C.F.R. 99.31 (a)(10) and 99.36. This exception to FERPA's general consent rule is limited to the period of the emergency and generally does not allow for a blanket release of personally identifiable information from a

[1] Available for download in brochure form at <www2.ed.gov/policy/gen/guid/fpco/brochures/elsec.html>.

student's education records. In addition, the Department interprets FERPA to permit institutions to disclose information from education records to parents if a health or safety emergency involves their son or daughter.

DISCIPLINARY RECORDS

While student disciplinary records are protected as education records under FERPA, there are certain circumstances in which disciplinary records may be disclosed without the student's consent. A postsecondary institution may disclose to an alleged victim of any crime of violence or non-forcible sex offense the final results of a disciplinary proceeding conducted by the institution against the alleged perpetrator of that crime, regardless of whether the institution concluded a violation was committed. An institution may disclose to anyone—not just the victim—the final results of a disciplinary proceeding, if it determines that the student is an alleged perpetrator of a crime of violence or non-forcible sex offense, and with respect to the allegation made against him or her, the student has committed a violation of the institution's rules or policies. *See* 34 C.F.R. 99.31 (a)(13) and (14).

THE CLERY ACT

The *Jeanne Clery Disclosure of Campus Security Policy and Campus Crime Statistics Act* requires postsecondary institutions to provide timely warnings of crimes that represent a threat to the safety of students or employees and to make public their campus security policies. It also requires that crime data be collected, reported and disseminated to the campus community and to the Department annually. The *Clery Act* is intended to provide students and their families with accurate, complete and timely information about safety on campuses so that they can make informed decisions. Such disclosures are permitted under FERPA. The following website provides more information about these and other provisions about campus safety: <ed.gov/admins/lead/safety/campus.html>.

LAW ENFORCEMENT UNIT RECORDS

Many colleges and universities have their own law enforcement units to monitor safety and security in and around campus. Institutions that do not have specific law enforcement units may designate a particular office or school official to be responsible for referring potential or alleged violations of law to local police authorities. Investigative reports and other records created and maintained by these law enforcement units are not considered education records subject to FERPA. Accordingly, institutions may disclose information from law enforcement unit records to anyone, including outside law enforcement authorities, without student consent. *See* 34 C.F.R. 99.8.

While an institution has flexibility in deciding how to carry out safety functions, it must also indicate in its policy or in information provided to students which office or school official serves as the college or university's "law enforcement unit." (The institution's notification to students of their rights under FERPA can include this designation. As an example, the Department has posted a model notification on its website at <ed.gov/policy/gen/guid/fpco/ferpa/ps-officials.html>.)

Law enforcement unit officials who are employed by the college or university should be designated in the institution's FERPA notification as "school officials" with a "legitimate educational interest." As such, they may be given access to personally identifiable information from students' education records. The institution's law enforcement unit officials must protect the privacy of education records it receives and may disclose them only in compliance with FERPA. For the reason, it is advisable that law enforcement unit records be maintained separately from education records.

DISCLOSURE TO PARENTS

When a student turns 18 years old or enters a postsecondary institution at any age, all rights afforded to parents under FERPA transfer to the student. However, FERPA also provides ways in which schools may share information with parents without the student's consent. For example:

- Schools may disclose education records to parents if the student is a dependent for income tax purposes.
- Schools may disclose education records to parents if a health or safety emergency involves their son or daughter.
- Schools may inform parents if the student who is under age 21 has violated any law or its policy concerning the use or possession of alcohol or a controlled substance.

- A school official may generally share with a parent information that is based on that official's personal knowledge or observation of the student.

FERPA AND STUDENT HEALTH INFORMATION

Postsecondary institutions that provide health or medical services to students may share student medical treatment records with parents under the circumstances described above. While these records may otherwise be governed by the *Health Insurance Portability and Accountability Act of 1996* (HIPAA), the HIPAA Privacy Rule excludes student medical treatment records and other records protected by FERPA.

The Education Department, along with the Department of Health and Human Services, issued joint updated guidance in December 2019 on the interplay between FERPA and HIPAA. The agencies revised guidance first issued in November 2008 to clarify for school administrators, health care professionals, families, and others how FERPA and HIPAA apply to education and health records maintained about students. In particular, the guidance addresses when a student's health information can be shared without the written consent of the parent or eligible student under FERPA, or without written authorization under the HIPAA Privacy Rule.

New clarifications and examples address:

- when protected health information (PHI) or personally identifiable information from an education record (PII) can be shared with the parent of a minor versus an adult student, including options family members of an adult student have under HIPAA if they are concerned about the student's mental health and the student does not agree to disclosures of their PHI;
- when PHI or PII can be shared about a student who presents a danger to self or others;
- when a school that employs a health care provider and conducts covered transactions electronically is subject to the FERPA privacy standards instead of the HIPAA privacy standards;
- when, under FERPA, an educational agency or institution can disclose, without prior written consent, PII from a student's education records, including health records, to the educational agency's or institution's law enforcement officials;

- when an educational agency or institution can disclose, without prior written consent, PII from a student's education records to the National Instant Criminal Background Check System (NICS); and
- when certain disclosures are allowed without the written consent of the parent or eligible student under FERPA or without authorization under the HIPAA Privacy Rule, especially those related to emergency health or safety situations.

Additional information and guidance may be found at: <studentprivacy.ed.gov/resources/joint-guidance-application-ferpa-and-hipaa-student-health-records>.

FERPA AND STUDENT AND EXCHANGE VISITOR INFORMATION SYSTEM (SEVIS)

FERPA permits institutions to comply with information requests from the Department of Homeland Security (DHS) and its Immigration and Customs Enforcement Bureau (ICE) in order to comply with the requirements of SEVIS. Officials who have specific questions about this and other matters involving international students should contact the U.S. Department of Education's Student Privacy Policy Office.

TRANSFER OF EDUCATION RECORDS

FERPA permits school officials to disclose any and all education records, including disciplinary records, to another institution at which the student seeks or intends to enroll. While student consent is not required for transferring education records, the institution's annual FERPA notification should indicate that such disclosures are made. In the absence of information about disclosures in the annual FERPA notification, school officials must make a reasonable attempt to notify the student about the disclosure, unless the student initiates the disclosure. Additionally, upon request, the institution must provide a copy of the information disclosed and an opportunity for a hearing. *See* 34 C.F.R. 99.31(a)(2) and 99.34(a).

Institutions implementing reverse transfer procedures must follow FERPA guidelines. In a reverse transfer, academic credits for coursework completed at a four-year institution are transferred back to a previously-attended two-year institution to satisfy an associate's degree or certification requirements. FERPA, under certain circumstances, waives the signed consent requirement. However, none of the exceptions currently apply to disclosures of completion information to institutions from which a student has transferred. Therefore, school officials must obtain signed consent from transferring students in order to disclose their education records to the two-year institution. While the student must provide a signed consent, the consent can reside with another party, such as the two-year institution, rather than the party providing the records. Alternatively, the four-year institution can include consent language in the admissions application as a separate item which states that the student permits disclosure of degree-qualifying records back to their previous institution. *See* 34 C.F.R. 99.30.

CONTACT INFORMATION

For further information about FERPA, please contact the Student Privacy Policy Office or visit its website.

Student Privacy Policy Office
U.S. Department of Education
400 Maryland Ave., S.W.
Washington, DC 20202-5901
(202) 260-3887

For quick, informal responses to routine questions about FERPA, school officials may email the Student Privacy Policy Office at <ferpa@ed.gov>.

For inquiries about FERPA compliance training, contact <ferpa.client@ed.gov>.

Additional information and guidance may be found at the SPPO website at: <ed.gov/policy/gen/guid/fpco/>.

APPENDIX F

GDPR FAQ

The information contained in this FAQ is not legal advice. If you have a legal issue related to EU Privacy or Data Protection, please contact a licensed attorney for guidance specific to your situation.

European regulatory authorities are slowly releasing guidance on the GDPR, which will help instruct how organizations can come into compliance.

The GDPR applies to the processing of personal data of data subjects. Who is covered by the GDPR—as a data controller, data processor, or data subject?

Article 3 of the GDPR establishes its "Territorial scope." The GDPR applies to:

- "[T]he processing of personal data in the context of the activities of an establishment of a controller or a processor in the Union, regardless of whether the processing takes place in the Union or not."
- "[T]he processing of personal data of data subjects who are in the Union by a controller or processor not established in the Union, where the processing activities are related to:
- the offering of goods or services, irrespective of whether a payment of the data subject is required, to such data subjects in the Union; or
- the monitoring of their behaviour as far as their behaviour takes place within the Union."
- "[T]he processing of personal data by a controller not established in the Union, but in a place where Member State law applies by virtue of public international law."

Does the GDPR apply to individuals who are in the EU on a temporary basis, for example enrolled in a study abroad program?

Yes, the GDPR applies to "the processing of personal data of data subjects who are in the Union."

The GDPR establishes obligations for data controllers and data processors. What is the difference? If third party vendors are selling products to university students, would they be considered controllers in that instance or still processors?

A data controller is the entity that determines the purposes and means of the processing of personal data. A data processor is an entity that processes personal data *only* on behalf of and on the instructions of the controller (*e.g.*, service providers).

Data controllers are subject to significantly more legal obligations under the GDPR than processors. Processors have some legal requirements, but most obligations will be contractual.

What must a controller do to engage a data processor under the GDPR? Can a third party deliver PII to the school under this regulation?

Controllers must enter into written agreements with processors that establish the "subject-matter and duration of the processing, the nature and purpose of the processing, the type of personal data and categories of data subjects and the obligations and rights of the controller," among other provisions established by Article 28 of the GDPR.

The GDPR requires that processing of personal data be done in accordance with a legal basis. What are the legal bases for processing personal data under the GDPR?

Article 6 sets out the legal bases for processing personal data under the GDPR, but they include:

- Consent;
- Processing necessary for the performance of a contract;
- Processing necessary for compliance with a legal obligation;
- Processing necessary to protect the vital interests of the data subject or of another natural person; and
- Processing necessary for the legitimate interests of the controller.

It is important to note that consent may be revoked by the data subject.

At what level of the institution is the legal basis for processing personal data determined? Is the legal basis for processing PII per office or institutionals the legal basis for processing PII per office or institutional? In other words, can there be blanket consent for all institutional operations, or is it only applicable for specific offices?

Controllers must identify the legal basis for each processing activity in which they are engaged.

With Brexit, is the United Kingdom covered by the GDPR?

The UK Government has signaled its intention to implement the GDPR. The UK Information Commissioner's Office continues to release guidance on complying with the GDPR.

Have U.S. legislators implemented legislation to align with the GDPR? I am still uncertain about how the EU will fine a U.S. college.

No, but pursuant to Article 3 of the GDPR, the "processing of personal data of data subjects who are in the Union by a controller or processor not established in the Union," may be subject to the GDPR.

What is the "right to be forgotten" and how does it work? What constitutes as a "legitimate" record that can be forgotten? Are there circumstances in which a request to be forgotten cannot be executed?

Article 17 of the GDPR provides data subjects with the "right to erasure" or the "right to be forgotten." The right is not absolute and the GDPR establishes the conditions under which a data subject can access this right.

Among other conditions, the data controller must erase and prevent the processing of personal data at an individual's request:

- If no longer necessary for original purpose for which it was collected;
- If the data subject withdraws consent;
- When the data subject objects to further processing and there is no overriding "legitimate interest" to continue processing;
- When data have been unlawfully processed;
- When necessary to comply with a legal obligation under Union or Member State law to which the controller is subject; and

- When related to the offer of "information society services" (*e.g.*, on-line platforms) to a child.

APPENDIX G

FERPA Guidance for Contracts and Written Agreements

Model University-Vendor Contracts that fit all of the guidance suggested below are available as an appendix item in the *2012 AACRAO FERPA Guide* or can be accessed online at <aacrao.org/docs/default-source/pubs/book-content/appendix-n-ferpa-guide>.

What is the Family Educational Rights and Privacy Act?

The Family Educational Rights and Privacy Act (FERPA), 20 U.S.C. §1232g, is a Federal privacy law administered by the Student Privacy Policy Office (SPPO or Office) in the U.S. Department of Education (Department or we). FERPA and its implementing regulations in 34 C.F.R. part 99 protect the privacy of students' education records and afford parents and eligible students (*i.e.*, students who are 18 years of age or older or attend an institution of postsecondary education) certain rights to inspect and review education records, to seek to amend these records, and to consent to the disclosure of personally identifiable information from education records (PII from education records).

The general rule under FERPA is that PII from education records cannot be disclosed without written consent. However, FERPA includes several exceptions that permit the disclosure of PII from education records without consent. Two of these exceptions are discussed in this document—the studies exception and the audit or evaluation exception. The two exceptions contain specific, and slightly different, requirements, described more fully in the implementing regulations (34 C.F.R. Part 99).

What is the purpose of this document?

The audience for this document includes schools, school districts (also referred to as local educational agencies (LEAs)), postsecondary institutions, and State educational authorities (such as State educational agencies (SEAs)) that may disclose PII from education records. Our intent is to provide these entities with information about requirements and best practices for data disclosures under the studies exception and the audit or evaluation exception.

What is the Studies Exception?
[*see* 20 U.S.C. §1232g(b)(1)(F) and §99.31(a)(6)]
The studies exception allows for the disclosure of PII from education records without consent to organizations conducting studies for, or on behalf of, schools, school districts, or postsecondary institutions. Studies can be for the purpose of developing, validating, or administering predictive tests; administering student aid programs; or improving instruction.

- Example : An SEA may disclose PII from education records without consent to an organization for the purpose of conducting a study that compares program outcomes across school districts to further assess what programs provide the best instruction and then duplicate those results in other districts.

What is the Audit or Evaluation Exception? [*see* 20 U.S.C. 1232g(b)(1)(C), (b)(3), and (b)(5) and §§99.31(a)(3) and 99.35]
The audit or evaluation exception allows for the disclosure of PII from education records without consent to authorized representatives of the Comptroller General of the U.S., the Attorney General, the Secretary of Education, and State or local educational authorities (FERPA-permitted entities). Under this exception, PII from education records must be used to audit or evaluate a Federal-or State-supported education program, or to enforce or comply with Federal legal requirements that relate to those education programs (audit, evaluation, or enforcement or compliance activity). The entity disclosing the PII from education records is specifically required to use reasonable methods to ensure to the greatest extent practicable that its designated authorized representative complies with FERPA and its regulations.

- Example : An LEA could designate a university as an authorized representative in order to disclose, without consent, PII from education records on its former students to the university. The university then may disclose, without consent, transcript data on these former students to the LEA to permit the LEA to evaluate how effectively the LEA prepared its students for success in postsecondary education.

How do you define education program?

"Education program" is an important term under the audit or evaluation exception because PII from education records can only be disclosed to audit or evaluate a Federal-or State-supported "education program," or to enforce or to comply with Federal legal requirements related to an education program. As specified in the FERPA regulations, §99.3, an education program must be principally engaged in the provision of education, including, but not limited to, early childhood education, elementary and secondary education, postsecondary education, special education, job training, career and technical education, and adult education, and any program that is administered by an educational agency or institution. For a definition of "early childhood program" please refer to §99.3 of the FERPA regulations.

Do we need to have a written agreement to disclose PII from education records without consent?

Yes. Both the studies exception and the audit or evaluation exception specifically require that the parties execute a written agreement when disclosing PII from education records without consent. The mandatory elements of that agreement vary slightly between the two exceptions.

Are there mandatory provisions for written agreements under the studies exception?

Yes. Written agreements under the studies exception must in accordance with the requirements in §99.31(a)(6)(iii)(C):

- Specify the purpose, scope, and duration of the study and the information to be disclosed. Your agreement must specify the purpose of the study, describe its scope and its duration, and identify the information being disclosed.
- Require the organization to use PII from education records only to meet the purpose or purposes of the study as stated in the written agreement. Your agreement must specify that the PII from education records must only be used for the study identified in the agreement.

- Require the organization to conduct the study in a manner that does not permit the personal identification of parents and students by anyone other than representatives of the organization with legitimate interests. Your agreement must require the organization to conduct the study so as not to identify students or their parents. This typically means that the organization should allow internal access to PII from education records only to individuals with a need to know, and that the organization should take steps to maintain the confidentiality of the PII from education records at all stages of the study, including within the final report, by using appropriate disclosure avoidance techniques.
- Require the organization to destroy all PII from education records when the information is no longer needed for the purposes for which the study was conducted, and specify the time period in which the information must be destroyed. Your agreement must require the organization to destroy the PII from education records when it is no longer needed for the identified study. You should determine the specific time period for destruction based on the facts and circumstances surrounding the disclosure and study. The parties to the written agreement may agree to amend the agreement to extend the time period if needed, but the agreement must include a time limit.

Are there mandatory provisions for written agreements under the audit or evaluation exception?

Yes. The mandatory provisions for written agreements under the audit or evaluation exception are similar to, but slightly different from, the provisions required for written agreements under the studies exception. Section 99.35(a)(3) specifically requires that the following provisions be included in written agreements under the audit or evaluation exception:

- Designate the individual or entity as an authorized representative. Your agreement must formally designate the individual or entity as an authorized representative.
- Specify the PII from education records to be disclosed. Your agreement must identify the information being disclosed.
- Specify that the purpose for which the PII from education records is being disclosed to the authorized representative is to carry out an audit or

evaluation of Federal-or State-supported education programs, or to enforce or to comply with Federal legal requirements that relate to those programs. Your agreement must state specifically that the disclosure of the PII from education records is in furtherance of an audit, evaluation, or enforcement or compliance activity.

- Describe the activity with sufficient specificity to make clear that it falls within the audit or evaluation exception. This must include a description of how the PII from education records will be used. Don't be vague—the agreement must describe the methodology and why disclosure of PII from education records is necessary to accomplish the audit, evaluation, or enforcement or compliance activity.
- Require the authorized representative to destroy the PII from education records when the information is no longer needed for the purpose specified. Your agreement should be clear about how the PII from education records will be destroyed.
- Specify the time period in which the PII must be destroyed. Your agreement must provide a time period for destruction. You should determine the specific time period for destruction based on the facts and circumstances surrounding the disclosure and activity. The parties to the written agreement may agree to amend the agreement to extend the time period if needed, but the agreement must include a time limit.
- Establish policies and procedures, consistent with FERPA and other Federal and State confidentiality and privacy provisions, to protect PII from education records from further disclosure (except back to the disclosing entity) and unauthorized use, including limiting use of PII from education records to only authorized representatives with legitimate interests in an audit, evaluation, or enforcement or compliance activity. The agreement must establish the policies and procedures, consistent with FEPRA and other Federal and State laws, to protect PII from education records from further disclosure or unauthorized use.

Can an entity receiving PII from education records disclose it in a way that allows individual students to be identified?

No. Absent consent from the parent or eligible student, FERPA provides that the PII from education records cannot be published in a way that would allow individual students and their parents to be identified. The organization conducting the study, audit, or evaluation can use PII from education records to conduct the study, audit, or evaluation, but results must be published in a way that protects the privacy and confidentiality of the individuals involved. For example, when publishing tables, cell suppression and other methods of disclosure avoidance can be used so that students cannot be identified through small numbers displayed in table cells.

Under the audit or evaluation exception, what is your responsibility to use "reasonable methods" to ensure that your authorized representative is FERPA-compliant to the greatest extent practicable? [§99.35(a)(2)]

When you disclose PII from education records under the audit or evaluation exception, you are required to use "reasonable methods" to ensure to the greatest extent practicable that your authorized representative is FERPA-compliant. This specifically means ensuring that your authorized representative does the following:

- Uses PII from education records only to carry out an audit or evaluation of Federal-or State-supported education programs, or for the enforcement of or compliance with, Federal legal requirements related to these programs. You should make sure that the proposed audit or evaluation is legitimate, and require in your written agreement that your authorized representative use the PII from education records only for that audit, evaluation, or enforcement or compliance activity. You should not disclose all of your PII from education records; rather, you should determine which specific elements your authorized representative needs and disclose only those.
- Protects the PII from education records from further disclosures or other uses, except as authorized by you in accordance with FERPA. Your agreement must specify that your authorized representative may not further disclose the PII from education records, unless authorized. Approval to use the PII from education records for one audit or evaluation does not confer approval to use it for another.
- Destroys the PII from education records when no longer needed for the audit, evaluation, or enforcement or compliance activity. Your agreement

must specify that your authorized representative is required to destroy the PII from education records when it is no longer needed and specify the time period in which the PII must be destroyed.

Are there best practices that support reasonable methods?

Yes. While it is vital for organizations to comply with FERPA and its regulations, FERPA represents the floor for protecting privacy, not the ceiling. Accordingly, the Department is also specifying best practices, in which we describe actions we recommend you take to ensure that your authorized representative is protecting privacy to the greatest extent possible. Best practices are broader than FERPA compliance and describe recommended actions you should take to ensure that your authorized representative is FERPA-compliant to the greatest extent practicable.

These best practices may apply to data sharing under both the audit and evaluation exception and the studies exception. Please keep in mind that not all of the following best practices are appropriate in every instance, and this list does not include every possible protection. Before disclosing PII from education records under one of these exceptions, you should examine the following list and tailor your practices as necessary and appropriate.

- *Convey the limitations on the data.* You should take steps to ensure your authorized representative knows the limitations on the use of the data (*i.e.*, that the data is only to carry out the audit or evaluation of Federal-or State-supported education programs, or to enforce or to comply with Federal legal requirements that relate to those programs).
- *Obtain assurances against redisclosure.* You should obtain assurances from your authorized representative that the data will not be redisclosed without permission, including such assurances that your authorized representative will provide you (the disclosing entity) the right to review any data prior to publication and to verify proper disclosure avoidance techniques have been used.
- *Be clear about destruction.* You should set clear expectations so your authorized representative knows what process needs to be followed for the proper destruction of PII from education records.

- *Maintain a right to audit.* You should maintain the right to conduct audits or other monitoring activities of your authorized representative's policies, procedures, and systems.
- *Verify the existence of disciplinary policies to protect data.* You may want to verify that your authorized representative has appropriate disciplinary policies for employees that violate FERPA. This can include termination in appropriate instances.
- *Verify the existence of a sound data security plan.* You may wish to verify before disclosing PII from education records that your authorized representative has a sound data security program, one that protects both data at rest and data in transmission. You have a responsibility to determine if your authorized representative's data security plan is adequate to prevent FERPA violations. The steps that you may need to take in order to verify a sound data security program are likely to vary with each situation. In some cases, it may suffice to add language to the written agreement that states what data security provisions are required. In other cases, it may be more prudent for you to take a hands-on approach and complete a physical inspection. Additionally, your written agreements could specify required data security elements, including requirements related to encryption, where the data can be hosted, transmission methodologies, and provisions to prevent unauthorized access.
- *Verify the existence of a data stewardship program.* You may want to examine your authorized representative's data stewardship program. Data stewardship should involve internal control procedures that protect PII from education records and include all aspects of data collection—from planning to maintenance to use and dissemination. The Department believes that a good data stewardship plan would have support and participation from across the organization, including the head of the organization, management, legal counsel, and data administrators, providers, and users. The plan should detail the organization's policies and procedures to protect privacy and data security, including the ongoing management of data collection, processing, storage, maintenance, use, and destruction. The plan could also include designating an individual to oversee the privacy and security of the PII from the education records it maintains. For more information, we have posted for comment a technical brief: "Data

Stewardship: Managing Personally Identifiable Information in Electronic Student Education Records" that can be found at <www2.ed.gov/policy/gen/guid/ptac/technical-briefs.html>.

- *Disclose only PII from education records that is needed.* When you consider disclosing PII from education records to an authorized representative for an audit, evaluation, or enforcement or compliance activity, you may want to explore which specific data elements are necessary for that activity and provide only those elements. You should take care to ensure that you are not disclosing more PII from education records than needed for the stated activity and purpose. You should also explore whether PII from education records is actually required, or whether de-identified data would suffice.
- *Know to whom you are disclosing data.* You may want to require your authorized representative to conduct background investigations of employees who will have access to PII from education records, or you may want to conduct these investigations yourself. Additionally, you may want to require your authorized representative to disclose past FERPA or data management violations. If you discover past violations, you would want to explore the circumstances behind the violation, and discover all information that would allow you to make an informed judgment on whether the individual or entity is likely to be a responsible data steward. This may include discovering whether the violation was covered up, including if it was voluntarily reported to affected students or SPPO, and whether appropriate breach response procedures were followed.
- *Verify training.* You may want to verify that your authorized representative has a training program to teach its employees about FERPA and how to protect PII from education records, or you may want to train your authorized representatives yourself.

Are there best practices for written agreements?

You should consider the following items for inclusion in your written agreements for work under both the audit or evaluation exception and the studies exception. We note that this list may not cover everything you want in your agreement—you should look to the facts and circumstances surrounding the disclosure agreement and include all terms necessary to be clear about roles, responsibilities, and expectations for safeguarding PII from education records.

- *Bind individuals to the agreement.* It can be important to bind not just the entity to whom you are disclosing PII from education records, but also the individuals who will be accessing that data. There are several ways to accomplish this result. One way is to identify the individuals in the agreement itself, and have them execute the agreement in their individual capacity as well as having a representative execute the agreement for the entity. Alternatively, your agreement can require individuals accessing the PII from education records to execute affidavits of nondisclosure or other documentation indicating their individual agreement to handle the PII from education records properly.
- *Agree on limitations on use of the PII from education records.* Your agreement should be clear about limitations on the use of the PII from education records, meaning that it can only be used for the activities described in the agreement. Your agreement may also address methodological limitations, for example, identifying which data sets, if any, the PII from education records may be linked.
- *Agree to not redisclose.* The most basic provision of the agreement is to make clear that the PII from education records is confidential and must not be redisclosed through direct data disclosures or publishing results that allow individuals to be directly or indirectly identified. FERPA-permitted entities may wish to require that specified disclosure avoidance methodologies be applied, or may wish to review all results prior to publication, or both.
- *Specify points of contact/data custodians.* Your written agreements should specify points of contact and data custodians (the individuals directly responsible for managing the data in question).
- *Mention Institutional Review Board (IRB) review and approval.* While FERPA does not mention IRBs, research proposals involving human subjects may have to be reviewed and approved by IRBs, if required under protection of human subject regulations of the Department and other Federal agencies. If IRB review and approval is required or expected, this may be noted in the written agreement.
- *State ownership of PII from education records.* You may wish for your agreement to be clear that, in disclosing PII from education records to an entity, you are in no way assigning ownership of the PII or records to that

entity, and that it may only be redisclosed with your permission or otherwise in compliance with FERPA and its regulations.

- *Identify penalties.* Your agreement could include penalties under State contract law such as liquidated damages, data bans of varying length, and any other penalties the parties to the agreement deem appropriate. You may want your agreement to create third-party beneficiary rights, *e.g.*, allowing parties injured by a data breach to sue for damages. While FERPA itself has little flexibility for sanctions, you can include a wide range of appropriate sanctions in your written agreements.
- *Set terms for data destruction.* As discussed previously, written agreements for both studies and audits and evaluations are required to contain provisions dealing with the destruction of PII from education records when those records are no longer needed. The agreement could include a method for documenting the destruction, such as the use of notarized statements.
- *Include funding terms.* If the agreement involves cost reimbursement, these details could be specified.
- *Maintain right to audit.* You may want to include the right to conduct audits or otherwise monitor the entity to which you are disclosing PII from education records to periodically affirm that the entity has appropriate policies and procedures in place to protect the PII from education records.
- *Identify and comply with all legal requirements.* It is important to remember that FERPA may not be the only law that governs your agreement. The agreement could broadly require compliance with all applicable Federal, State, and local laws and regulations, and identify the legal authority (whether express or implied) that permits the audit, evaluation, or enforcement or compliance activity.
- *Have plans to handle a data breach.* While no one anticipates a data breach, data loss may occur. You may wish to include specific procedures in your written agreements detailing the parties' expectations in the event that PII from education records is lost, including specifying the parties' responsibilities with regard to breach response and notification and financial responsibility.
- *Review and approve reported results.* If applicable, the written agreement could specify the parties' agreements with respect to publication of results. For example, you may wish to review and approve reports prior to

publication to make sure that they reflect the original intent of the agreement.

- *Define terms for conflict resolution.* The agreement could specify procedures for how disputes between the parties would be resolved.
- *Specify modification and termination procedures.* The agreement could specify how it can be modified or terminated. You may wish to provide specific provisions for termination based on improper handling of PII from education records.

What do I do if the terms of the written agreement are violated?

If the entity to which you have disclosed PII from education records without consent (whether under the studies exception or the audit an evaluation exception) violates the terms of the written agreement, you should evaluate your options under the penalty and termination provisions of the agreement. You may want to stop disclosing PII from education records to that organization, or pursue legal redress. If you have reason to believe that the entity has violated FERPA, you should contact SPPO.

How should the public be informed?

It is a best practice to keep the public informed when you disclose PII from education records.

- *Inform the public about written agreements.* Transparency is a best practice. You might want to post your data sharing agreements on your website, or provide some equivalent method to let interested parties know what data you are disclosing, the reasons it is being disclosed, and how it is being protected. While the Department generally recommends public posting of written agreements, parties are encouraged to review their contractual data security provisions carefully and redact, prior to publication, any provisions that may aid those seeking unauthorized access to systems. In certain instances a separate confidential IT Security Plan may be appropriate. For more information on data security best practices, see the Privacy Technical Assistance Center (PTAC) website: <www2.ed.gov/policy/gen/guid/ptac/>.

Who should I call if I have questions?

If you would like more information about best practices to protect PII from education records, contact the PTAC Help Desk at <PrivacyTA@ed.gov> or (855) 249-3072.

If you are a parent, eligible student, school, LEA, or SEA and would like more information on FERPA, please call SPPO at (202) 260-3887.

APPENDIX H

True/False Quiz & Answer Key

The following tool might be used as a "teaser" to provide a sense of a person's familiarity/comfort level with FERPA, as well as a training tool. Pick and choose items based on time available and/or how the instrument is being utilized.

Answers to this quiz can be found at the end of this chapter on page 139.

1. __ "Education records" include only those records contained in a student's permanent file.
2. __ Students must be given the opportunity to inspect and review their education records within 10 days of a request.
3. __ Faculty has the right to inspect and review the education records of any student.
4. __ If a student discloses in an open forum that he has been suspended and that he feels the suspension is unwarranted, the school may infer that he has given implied consent for openly discussing the issue.
5. __ An adviser does not have to allow a student to inspect and review her personal notes about the student that are held in a file in the desk of the adviser's office.

6. __ The institution doesn't need to provide access to the educational records of a student to a non-custodial parent if the custodial parent submits a notarized statement that he or she does not consent to the disclosure.

7. __ A school does not have to send education records to another school in which a student seeks or intends to enroll if the student has an outstanding balance to the current institution.

8. __ A student has the right to inspect and review an essay submitted by the student, even if the teacher does not intend to return it to the student or to permanently maintain it.

9. __ Health records, maintained at the student health center, are education records, subject to FERPA.

10. __ A college newspaper has the right of access to detailed information about disciplinary hearings for students at the institution.

11. __ A state institution in Ohio must respond to a subpoena received from the Supreme Court of California.

12. __ An institution should provide data to an engineering firm which asks for a list of all the College of Engineering students who are in the top 10 percent of the senior class.

13. __ Tom Faculty has posted the grades of all the students in his class on the wall outside his office. This is a violation of FERPA.

14. __ Sally Student, who is not a dependent student, has been found in violation of the university's residence halls' alcohol policies. Her hall director could contact her parents to discuss the violation without her permission.

15. __ Admissions records are "education records," therefore covered under FERPA.

16. __ A student's social security number (SSN) could be verified to a caller who received a document with the student's SSN on it.

17. __ Ralph Student feels that his college records have been released inappropriately. Ralph can use FERPA to bring a suit against the college.

18. __ Tom Terrific graduated from State University several years ago. He has been very involved as an alumnus. A journalism student wants to write a story about his involvement at the university, both as a student and as an alumnus. The university should release only his alumni information.

19. __ Using the institutional student ID number (SIN), Tom Faculty has posted the grades of all the students in his class on the wall outside his office. This is violation of FERPA.

20. __ "Student recruiting information" under the Solomon Amendment is the same as "directory information" under FERPA.

True/False Quiz Answer Key

Q	A	Notes
1	F	With specific exceptions, "education records" are those maintained by the institution in any format that is identifiable to the student.
2	F	While institutions legally have 45 days to respond, consider whether you prefer and are able to fulfill the request in a more timely fashion, and whether your state open records law identifies a more abbreviated time frame for response.
3	F	All faculty and staff must show a "legitimate educational interest/need to know" within the context of their role to have appropriate access to education records.
4	F	There is no implied consent in FERPA, so you need to follow regular guidelines for releasing this student record information.
5	T	"Sole possession" records are an exception to the definition of "education records," and are therefore not accessible by the student.
6	F	If the student is legally financially dependent on either parent, then either parent can submit a request to access the student's record. If the institution would provide access for one parent, it may do so for either parent.
7	T	While the institution must provide access to the student, it is not required to do so for any third party.
8	T	So long as the record currently exists, it would be part of the student's "education record" and the student has the right to access it.
9	F	Medical treatment records are not covered by FERPA, so long as they are shared only with other medical service providers.
10	F	If the student is found in violation of the institution's conduct code related to a "crime of violence," then the student's name, violation and result of the disciplinary hearing are public information—releasable to anyone. Detailed disciplinary records are never public information, and the names of any victims or witnesses cannot be disclosed without consent.

T=True, F=False, D=Depends

Q	A	Notes
11	F	A state court has legal jurisdiction only within that state. However, it is permissible for the institution in Ohio to respond to the California subpoena as a matter of professional courtesy. All the FERPA requirements regarding responding to subpoenas must be followed.
12	F	There are three issues here. First, grades and GPAs can never be directory information. Academic honors (*e.g.*, Dean's List) can be directory information if the school has so designated academic honors to fall in that category. The question of top 10% of grades falls into a somewhat gray area, since it does not directly provide access to grade information for an individual student, but also does not meet the definition of directory information. In fact, it may come close to identifying grade information. Our recommendation is that schools not release the names of students in a top category of grades if that category is not designated as an academic honor in directory information.
13	D	It depends on HOW he posted the grades. If by name, Student ID Number, SSN (or part thereof), or something that can be fairly easily interpreted by a third party, then "yes," it's a violation. However, if the grades were posted by some "code" known only by the student and instructor, then that's OK.
14	T	This is true for any student under the age of 21—regardless of whether or not the student is financially dependent on their parent. Note that some state laws prohibit sharing this information without permission.
15	D	If the student is not yet "in attendance," then records related to the admission would generally not be an "education record." This is also true if the student is never admitted. However, if admitted and enrolled, all admissions records the institution continues to maintain become education records. It is also important that institutions familiarize themselves with state law and when education records start under those provisions since some begin once an institution begins creating a record.
16	F	A student's social security number can never be directory information, and therefore cannot be disclosed or even confirmed as public information.
17	F	There is no private cause of action under FERPA. This issue was confirmed by the U.S. Supreme Court in *Gonzaga University v. John Doe*, a 2002 decision. The student might want to pursue action under a Common Law or state law remedy, such as libel or slander.
18	F	The 2009 regulations clarified that records created after the student was enrolled are considered Alumni Records and are generally open to the public because they are not "education records" under FERPA. Since this is a state school, the state's open records law may apply if FERPA does not. Unless the student has a "No Release" on his record, you could also release directory information about Tom from when he was a student.
19	T	Posting grades in any personally identifiable format, such as with a name, SSN or SIN, would be a violation under FERPA.
20	F	"Student Recruiting Information" is a set of data defined within the Solomon Amendment. "Directory information" is a set of data defined by each institution. While there MAY be substantial overlap among the data items at any specific institution, they are not the same.

T=True, F=False, D=Depends

References

AACRAO. 2018. *Implications of the General Data Protection Regulation: An Interassociation Guide*. Washington, D.C.: Author.

Rooker, L., and T. Falkner. 2012. *2012 FERPA Guide*. AACRAO. Washington, D.C.: American Association of Collegiate Registrars and Admissions Officers.

Locklin, T. 2020. What you should know about the new California Consumer Privacy Act. *AACRAO Connect*. February 24. Available at: <aacrao.org/resources/newsletters-blogs/aacrao-connect/article/what-you-should-know-about-the-new-california-consumer-privacy-act>.